MODERN GREENHOUSE METHODS: VEGETABLES

Other books by the same author:
Modern Greenhouse Methods: Flowers and Plants

MODERN GREENHOUSE METHODS: VEGETABLES

Ian Walls

FREDERICK MULLER LIMITED, LONDON

First published in Great Britain 1982 by
Frederick Muller Limited, Dataday House,
Alexandra Road, London SW19 7JU.

Copyright © 1982 by Ian Walls

All rights reserved. No part of this publication may
be reproduced, stored in a retrieval system, or transmitted,
in any form or by any means, electronic, mechanical,
photocopying, recording or otherwise, without the prior
consent of Frederick Muller Limited.

British Library Cataloguing in Publication Data

Walls, Ian
   Modern greenhouse methods: vegetables.
   1. Vegetable gardening 2. Greenhouse management
   I. Title
   635.0483 SB352
ISBN 0 584 10388 3

Printed in Great Britain by The Anchor Press Ltd., Essex

Contents

page

Introduction   **9**
    Economic Data. Heat Conversion. Marketing and Cultural Techniques.

Chapter One   **Tomatoes**   **13**
    Introduction, Botanical – Crop Statistics, Where to Grow, Seasons of Production, Timetable.

Chapter Two   **Systems of Growing Tomatoes**   **19**
    Border Growing, Grafted Plants, Module Growing, Hydroponics, Hybrid Systems, Straw Bales, Summary Table.

Chapter Three   **The Propagation Stage of Tomatoes**   **25**
    Plant Raising by Specialists. Seed Sowing, Germination, Composts, Light Treatment, Capillary Benches.

Chapter Four   **Growing On Tomatoes**   **31**
    Temperature Patterns, Spacing, Watering and Feeding Young Plants, Plant Raising Guide, Carbon Dioxide Enrichment. Grafting Tomatoes.

Chapter Five   **Planning for Planting Tomatoes**   **39**
    Difference in Costs of Three Systems of Growing. Selection Table.

Chapter Six   **Border Cultivation of Tomatoes**   **43**
    Soil Analysis and Interpretation of Results.

Chapter Seven   **Preparation of Borders for Tomatoes**   **47**
    Base Feeds, Plant Spacing, Timetable for Border Systems, Modular Systems, Rock Wool Systems, Straw Bales, Other Systems.

Chapter Eight   **Planting of Tomatoes**   **55**
    Establishment, Environmental Control, Early Treatment, Summary.

Chapter Nine	**Plant Training of Tomatoes**	**59**

Growing, Watering and Feeding, Picking, Finishing.

Chapter Ten	**Crop Economics of Tomatoes**	**67**
Chapter Eleven	**Pest and Disease Check for Tomatoes**	**71**
Chapter Twelve	**Cucumbers**	**75**

History, Statistics, Crop Timing, Sowing Procedure, Potting, Preparation of Growing Quarters, Nutritional Standards, Planting, Training, Water Needs, Mulching and Necking Up, Harvesting, Crop Economics, Pest and Disease Check.

Chapter Thirteen	**Lettuce Under Glass or Plastic**	**89**

Frames and Cloches. Historical and Botanical, Statistics, Enterprise Selection. Seed Facts, Programme for Production. Composts for Propagation. Nutritional Standards. Preparation for Crop. Sowing Pelleted Seed in Peat/Blocks, Large-scale Plant Propagation, Spacings, Seasonal Procedures, Crop Economics. Lettuce in Plastic Structures, Frames and Mobile Glasshouses. Pest and Disease Check.

Chapter Fourteen	**Other Vegetables**	**107**

Aubergines, Beans, Climbing French, Dwarf French, Runner, Beetroot, Brassicas, Carrots, Celery, Chinese Cabbage, Chicory, Cress, Endive, Gherkins, Herbs, Kohlrabi, Leeks, Marrows and Courgettes, Melons, Mushrooms, Onions and Leeks in Blocks, Parsley, Rhubarb, Radish, Sweet Peppers, Seakale, Sweet Corn.

Chapter Fifteen	**Nutrient Film Techniques and Rock Wool Systems**	**135**
Chapter Sixteen	**Plant Foods**	**149**

Soil/Substrate, Tissue Analysis, Liquid Fertilizers, Soil Sterilization.

Chapter Seventeen	**Composts**	**171**

Seed and Potting Composts. Physical Texture – Peat, Sand or Grit, Soil or Loam, Other Materials. Nutrient Supply. Pests, Diseases and Weeds. Selection of Compost Type. Re-cycling of Waste Compost. Self-formulation or Ready-mixed Composts. Costings Chemicals used in Composts, Compost Formulae, Soilless Composts, Base Fertilizers, Slow-release Fertilizers, Rates of Use – Seed Sowing and Cutting. Potting Composts, Blocking Composts, Fertilizer Requirements for Peat Blocking Composts. Conversion Table, Practical Aspects of Mixing Compost.

Appendix	**List of Firms Supplying Seeds**	**187**
Acknowledgements		**189**

List of Illustrations

		page
Figure 1	Grafting tomatoes is a technique which is certain to regain favour as it avoids the high costs of soil sterilization.	36
Figure 2	Spacing plants depends much on arrangement of heating pipes, width and height of greenhouse or structure and other considerations. This spacing is generally acceptable.	50
Figure 3	Bolsters or grow bags for double cropping can be arranged on several permutations aimed at minimum output of labour and maximum yields.	52
Figure 4	'Coathangers' are useful for holding spare twine on layering systems.	60
Figure 5	Plant training systems take many forms: 5a Plants taken up to wire and then layered by undoing and re-tying twine 5b As (5a) but using S hooks (or 'coathangers') 5c Arch systems 5d Layering from outset on vertical and horizontal twine or nets (nets used on Continent)	61
Figure 6	Training system for cucumbers 6a Training on arch systems 6b Vertical string method 6c 'V' systems	82
Figure 7	Nutrient Film Technique typical lay-out. (By kind permission of Nutriculture Ltd., Sandy Lane, Ormskirk.)	138
Figure 8	Rock wool system – typical lay-out	146

Plate section between pp 88–89

Introduction

The cultivation of vegetable crops under protection of glasshouses or plastics has seen considerable change in cultural techniques in recent years.

This is especially so in temperate zones where the rapid escalation in fuel prices has had a dramatic effect on the economic viability of cropping.

There have been many changes in the design and environmental control of glasshouses and plastic structures, all aimed at increasing their productive capacity – and maximizing return on capital investment. This has been linked to more precise cultural systems, with floods of new varieties of vegetables capable in some instances of year-round production.

Profound changes in attitude by the whole protected cropping industry have been necessary to cope with the increasing output of vegetable crops in tropical climate countries – which can be readily transported to temperate zones under controlled environmental conditions.

This book is intended as a practical, up-to-date look at the current protected cropping scene for growers and students.

I am deeply grateful to my many grower friends and colleagues in Britain and overseas for the help they have given me with the writing of this book.

Economic Data

I have made every effort to collate production costs and relate these realistically to returns, from the miscellany of varied information available and from different costing methods used by economists. It is my view that perhaps the most practical method is the Dutch system of calculating outputs and inputs per square metre and reducing this to rudimentary figures for *all* crops. Such systems do operate in the U.K. but diversity of unit size and cropping programmes make it difficult to

Introduction

present these costs in standard form which remain meaningful in the face of inflationary trends. All income figures refer to *gross income*, from which must be deducted marketing charges (this includes vehicle depreciation, etc.) and direct production quantities on a norm basis – per sq yd/sq m.

'Labour units'

Labour units relate to worker output on a man (or woman) hour on the following basis:

Worker Output

Regular Hours – (49 weeks per year)
  40 hours per week = 150 hours per month (average)
  1800 hours per year

'Labour Units'	'Crop' Area
* .1 sq yd (or metres) per man hour =	180 sq yd (or metres) per crop (or year)
* .5 sq yd (or metres) per man hour =	900 sq yd (or metres) per crop (or year)
1 sq yd (or metres) per man hour =	1800 sq yd (or metres) per crop (or year)
1.5 sq yd (or metres) per man hour =	2700 sq yd (or metres) per crop (or year)
2 sq yd (or metres) per man hour =	3600 sq yd (or metres) per crop (or year)
3 sq yd (or metres) per man hour =	4400 sq yd (or metres) per crop (or year)
* e.g. .7 sq yd = 900 + 180 + 180 =	1260 sq yd (or metres)

So man requirements per acre/ha are as follows:
  .5 sq yd per 'man' hour = 900 sq yd (or metres)
so 1 acre requires $^{4840}/_{900}$ = 5 'men'
  1 ha requires $^{10,000}/_{900}$ = 11 'men'

E.g. early heated tomatoes work out at $^{4840}/_{1800}$ = 2.8 workers per acre which is the generally accepted figure of 3 full-time workers with their overtime or with casuals (*less* if 7-day working weeks are considered).

Crop involvement is however seldom on a full-year basis and varies greatly from month to month.

It must also be appreciated that capital costs (on a depreciation basis), rent, rates, wages, including N.H.I., must all be costed against the enterprise. Interest on capital must also be allowed for.

Crop Losses

Few, if any, crops realize 100%. A figure of 80–85% is more realistic.

Expenses

Telephone, rates, house repairs, car and van upkeep must all be charged against a business.

Ian G. Walls
1982

Note on Heat Conversion

The economic notes in this book refer for convenience to *average* oil usage. For growers using coal, gas, wood, straw or other heat sources (waste heat, solar heat, heat pumps etc.) note that conversions will be required based on the *average* calorific value or output of the fuel sources.

Note that:
- 1 gallon of oil = 162,000 btu
- 1 litre of oil = 35,635 btu
- 1 lb of coal = 12,000 btu
- 1 kg of coal = 26,000 btu
- 1 kw of electricity = 3,412 btu

Gas sold on calorific value or on a volume and weight basis (check with supply source).
ALL LESS LOSS OF EFFICIENCY ON COMBUSTION*
Btu is now expressed as kilo joule kJ
1 btu = 1.055 kJ
1 kilocalorie = 4.186 kJ

You buy *more* gas to offset this.

Marketing and Cultural Techniques

The author has made detailed reference to the many sophisticated marketing techniques now being developed. These involve pre-packing cold storage (including ice banks) and other developments.

Cultural techniques are also changing constantly. The trade papers, research establishments and seed firms listed in the Appendix are excellent of the latest information.

Chapter One

Tomatoes

Introduction

The tomato is the most widely grown and popular vegetable crop under protection in temperate zones and out of doors in warm climates. It is a native of tropical America, having been eaten by the people of Mexico and called *tomati*. Matthiolus talks about the tomato in Italy around 1554 and while it was known in Europe prior to 1600 it was grown mainly as an ornamental plant until the latter part of the 18th century. Tomatoes first became popular as an edible vegetable in America in the late 18th century but it was not until towards the middle of the 19th century that they became widely grown principally for culinary purposes. Tomatoes are in the natural order *solanceae* and they belong to the genus *lycopersicon* (to which potatoes belong). According to Bailey (1924) there are several varieties of *I. esculentum*.

> commune – common tomato
> grandiflorum – large leaf tomato
> validum – upright tomato
> cerasiforme – cherry tomato
> pyriforme – pear tomato.

Since tomatoes were first categorized there has been much more segregation of sub-species in relation to gene counts (to exploit fruiting habits and encourage pest/disease resistance). The tomato is a highly nutritious vegetable and properly grown and picked at the correct stage, i.e. mature green and beyond, it should have a high sugar/low acid content. The longer the fruit can be left on the plant to ripen the higher the sugar/acid ratio and the sweeter the fruit. Many tomatoes reaching the U.K. in the winter period, especially from warmer areas, have a low sugar content and a tough leathery skin because, due to the distance they have to be transported, they are picked far too soon and ripen under bad conditions. Rising fuel costs have, in the 1980s, seen a move towards more and more production in warmer countries.

As far as the U.K. is concerned this means the Mediterranean zone and particularly Greece, Spain, Portugal, Tunisia, Morocco and other countries bordering the Mediterranean. Relative production figures in the E.E.C. and E.E.C.-pending countries (1979) are as follows:

Britain	120,000 tonnes
Belgium, Luxembourg	150,000 tonnes
Denmark	20,000 tonnes
France	600,000 tonnes
Germany	33,000 tonnes
Holland	3,180,000 tonnes
Ireland	27,000 tonnes
Italy	3,180,000 tonnes
TOTAL	7,310,000 tonnes
E.E.C.-Pending Countries (1979)	
Greece	1,380,000 tonnes
Spain	2,400,000 tonnes
Portugal	1,200,000 tonnes
TOTAL	4,980,000

The production figures under protection for 1981 (provisional) quoted by the MAFF for the United Kingdom were 128,600 tonnes from a production area of 2,137 acres (865 hectares).

In addition vast areas of glass and plastic are being erected in non-E.E.C. countries, such as Hungary, Rumania and North Africa for the production of tomatoes and other glasshouse crops. The tomato owes its popularity to a combination of succulence and nutrition value. There is little relationship between population and quantities produced by any country as there is vast export from warmer countries to the colder ones from the Mediterranean northwards. There has been a decline in tomato acreage in the U.K. during the late 1970s due to the rising production costs, principally fuel and labour. Increased efficiency of remaining producers has seen vastly bigger yields for a given area, well in excess of 100 tons per acre (250 tonnes/ha) for top growers. These increased yields are largely due to a combination of:

1 Modern light-admitting glasshouse structures of high gutter height which permits mechanized working. Multi Bay plastics with fan ventilators are also suitable.

Tomatoes 15

2 Varieties of high-yielding potential with certain inbred resistance to crop-restricting diseases and pests.
3 Training methods which allow stem extension and growth over a long period.
4 Pest- and disease-free substrates – or growing media.
5 Precise day/night temperatures regimes carefully given to a 'blueprint' pattern to give optimum yields.
6 Precise attention to requirements of plant food and water.
7 Additional yield boosting techniques such as carbon dioxide enrichment of the atmosphere and disease and pest control.

Where to Grow Tomatoes

In endeavouring to satisfy the above criteria, a modern, large pane glasshouse or plastic structure located in a good natural light area, without if possible an excessive exposure problem, is desirable. In many instances, however, existing conditions can fall far short of the ideal. New developments should as far as possible be planned in full knowledge of what conditions *should* be, as yields are critical to economic viability in temperate climates. Provision of services and, if possible, natural gas supplies are essential. It is interesting to note that the success and expansion in recent years of the tomato industry in the Hook of Holland is largely due to the high concentration of glasshouses in a coastal area generally of good natural light with pipe supplies of natural gas and ability to swing to oil should supplies be interrupted. There are of course other issues such as low interest loans, lower fuel costs, etc., in Holland and other countries.

Seasons of Production (Northern Europe)

	J	F	M	A	M	J	J	A	S	O	N	D
Early			―――――――――――――――――――
Mid				――――――――――――――
Late					―――――――――
Early/Late			――――――――			――――――

Timing of production conforms broadly to the timetable which follows, bearing in mind the variables introduced by the lower light intensities in many northern regions.

Enterprise Selection

There must be very careful consideration given to production region; the effect this has on fuel type and demands; projected yields; last but not least market outlets – whether wholesale, to markets and retail

16 Tomatoes

shops or direct marketing to the public – the last named only being practical on a limited production scale.

Costing of any project is essential – a matter discussed later – *bearing in mind that updating of costings is essential.* Costs which are given (see page 69) show Scotland to be at a big disadvantage for fuel (oil) usage, but generally higher prices per crop are obtained.

Waste Heat

The future for many glasshouse enterprises, especially for heat-loving crops such as tomatoes, will probably lie in the utilization of industrial waste or rejected heat – provided this is available in a good natural light area and on a constant basis.

Timetable of Production

Crop	Seed sowing	Potting	Spacing out	Planting	Picking	Comments
Early (no light)	Mid-end Nov.	End Nov. End Dec.	On three occasions as required	1–3rd week Feb. (according to natural light levels)	Mid Mar- early April	*Only* for good light areas.
Early Supplementary Light	Late Nov- early Dec.	Early-late Dec. Give light for 17–21 days	On three occasions as necessary	Mid Jan- early Feb.	Mid Mar- mid Apr.	Demands good light and modern facilities.
Second Early	Early-mid Dec.	Late Dec- early Jan.	On three occasions as for early crop but note light treatment period (see page 29)	Early Feb- early Mar.	Late Apr- early May	Still only a crop for the really well-equipped grower in a good light area.
Mid Season	Late Dec- early Jan.	Mid Jan.	On three occasions	Mid Mar- early Apr.	Early-mid May	A crop for the grower with a well-heated greenhouse.
Late	Mid Feb onwards	Late Feb	Twice as required	Mid-late April	June	The ideal crop for the less intense grower unprepared to invest highly in the crop with moderate or no heat.
Later or Cold	Early-mid Mar until Apr into early June for double cropping	Late Mar- early Apr or later	Twice as required	May-June- July	July – on	A favourite crop for the 'part-time' grower but growing season is greatly curtailed.

Tomatoes 17

Note:

In Holland and increasingly in the U.K., double cropping with early followed by a very late crop is practised to give a longer period of supply into the autumn months. There is also thought to be less labour involved in crop training and general management. Some growers also aim by double cropping to avoid marketing crops during the August period when the prices are poor. If continuity of cropping is demanded it is a question of sacrificing a portion of the early crop. Even at the best and with an extended season by double cropping into the autumn, there is a gap for temperate zone production, ranging from around November or December into March – a period of some four to five months. There is still crop involvement, however, as propagation goes on during November to January, and this is followed by a growing period from January until March until cropping starts again for the first early crop. Astute growers also 'bench' ripen crops to extend marketing.

British and Dutch growers are now setting up production units in the Mediterranean zone for early production – using their 'home' units for later cropping.

Chapter Two

Systems of Growing Tomatoes

With any crop which must be grown efficiently, there are invariably many different ways of crop management related to the circumstances.

(1) Border Growing

If there is a 'standard method' of growing tomatoes it relates to their culture in greenhouse soil borders. History shows this to be the first method employed for large-scale growing under protection. Renewal of the soil in the greenhouse border by hand or later by tractors was first of all practised in the early part of the century when labour was cheap. Eventually, however, it became necessary to evolve methods of leaving the soil 'in situ' and this brought soil sterilization much into vogue, in the early 1930s. At that time soil sterilization by steam was a tremendous step forward as a means of overcoming the mono-cultural problems associated with tomatoes, principally deep-seated root rots, eelworm and virus disease. In the 1980s large areas of tomatoes are still grown in greenhouse borders but there can be no doubt that other systems have made a big impact. This is for a variety of reasons, mostly related to economics and dependable high yields, overcoming pests and diseases with their crop-reducing effects, coupled with the high labour costs and weaknesses of soil sterilization methods, even at their best. Nevertheless the more newly developed systems of tomato culture such as module growing and nutrient film culture (NFT) (see Chapter 15) demand much more precise management than border growing. High costs are forcing growers back to border growing in the 1980s.

(2) Grafted Plants in Borders

This is basically the same as border growing (without sterilization) with

Systems of Growing Tomatoes

the difference that the selected varieties are grafted on to root stocks having inbred resistances to certain pests and diseases.

(3) 'Module' Growing

From a welter of systems involving, as they did, peat beds, peat mattresses with whale hide pots on top of peat beds and other miscellaneous systems, bolsters or grow bags containing a peat growing medium emerged in the late 1970s as the major cultural systems in many parts of the U.K. The greenhouse floor or border is best isolated from the crop completely with a continuous phase of black/white polythene, put down white upwards for light reflection and as a disease/weed barrier. The grow bags are then placed on top of the polythene, either 'on the flat' or on shallow depressions. This latter system can be combined with a layer of capillary matting on which suitably perforated bags are placed, when *all* water and feeding requirements are applied to the matting by various means and not the bolsters or grow bags. Where capillary matting is not used, trickle systems of watering and feeding are employed (to the bags). While commercial interests by the larger peat companies have boosted the bolster system, there can be no doubt that results have been on a very high order where meticulous cultural practices are carried out, with special reference to watering and feeding techniques. Porous bags are now used on capillary matting. Peat boards are also being used (VAPO) – this is compressed peat which expands when moist.

(4) Substrates Other Than Peat

The Netherlands has in recent years (late 1970s) become very involved in mineral rock wool cultural systems (Grodan). Mineral rock wool is a material widely used in the building industry for insulation purposes. A whole range of sizes of different and complementary pots or cubes are used from the seedling to the planting out stage. Here slabs of the rock wool wrapped in polythene to prevent algae growth are laid down in a similar way to bolsters or grow bags. One advantage is that rock wool readily lends itself to effective and complete sterilization by heat and can therefore be re-used. Precise watering and feeding techniques are necessary during cropping. Aggregates such as Perlite, which is an expanded volcanic ash, can readily be contained in polythene bags. Perlite can also be sterilized as it is a relatively inert material. Shredded wood bark (composted) and sawdust has also been used in troughs, either separately or mixed with peat. Clean ashes which can be available in certain districts in vast supplies have also been experimented with.

Systems of Growing Tomatoes 21

(5) Hydroponics (See Chapter 15, N.F.T.)
There has, in the U.K. and around the world generally, been considerable interest in hydroponic systems, especially, in recent years, the nutrient film technique (N.F.T.) This method was originally developed at the Glasshouse Crops Research Institute (G.C.R.I.), Littlehampton, Sussex (Dr. Alan Cooper). Careful evaluation of N.F.T. by research stations, growers and commercial firms such as I.C.I. has shown the possibility of very high yields. This is especially so where very careful monitoring and preferably automatic injection of nutrients and adjustment of pH have been the rule. N.F.T. is certainly not a method for the imprecise – although more definite rules can now be given which reduce the 'risk' factor and tomatoes have remarkable tolerance!

(6) 'Hybrid Systems'
As always with any crop, a mixture of cultural approaches tends to develop, largely conditioned by the scale of operations and materials to hand. Ring culture, where plants in 9 or 10 in (225–250 cm) bitumised paper pots containing a John Innes Compost are placed on top of a 5–6 in (125–150 cm) layer of weathered ash is a perfectly satisfactory system for the smaller scale grower. Likewise plants can be contained in the whale hide pots directly on top of doubtful unsterilized borders and this may be satisfactory for short season crops under less intensive conditions. Better still would be the placing of the whale hide pots on top of polythene, their bases on and surrounded by a mulch of peat.

Other cultural systems are at the development stage, including growing 'troughs' of various sorts.

(7) Straw Bale and Straw Wad Systems
Plants are grown on composted straw, isolated from pests and diseases by polythene. These are methods which are only practised spasmodically because they lack commercial 'push' as there is no large-scale purchase of growing accoutrements. In addition straw has tended to become a dear and variable commodity and can sometimes be chemically contaminated with weedkillers. Results can be superb with very high yields as shown by research stations (Lee Valley E.H.S. 1966 onwards) and growers.

(8) Aeroponic Systems
Systems where crops, including tomatoes, are grown in large platformed polythene tubes – with their roots surrounded by a 'fog' of nutrient – are at the development stage, especially in warm climates.

Systems of Growing Tomatoes

Summary Table

Method of Growing	For	Against
(1) Border growing	A stable way of culture with less critical demands for water and feeding than most other systems. Under the best conditions yields could be very high, of excellent quality 'natural' fruit.	Border soil very slow to warm up, which can result in planting late and subsequent root rots, especially when water seeps in from outdoors and chills the borders further. Quantities of water and feeding given to the plants difficult to control which makes plant growth tricky, especially following sterilization of the borders by heat. Build up of pests, diseases and 'soil sickness' occurs despite sterilization. Sterilization is an expensive and laborious process by heat although much less so with chemicals.
(2) Border growing with grafted plants	As above, with the added advantage of inbred resistance to certain root rots and other troubles thus enabling excellent crops to be grown in unsterilized soil. (It should be noted that a number of resistances are now incorporated into varieties.)	Grafting is both tedious and costly. The spread of virus disease can be a problem, although virus resistance root stock is available.
(3) Module growing	A clean start, at reasonable but rising investment, in relatively small quantities of growing media provided the growing media is well structured and this applies especially to peat. Provided watering/feeding is meticulously attended to, results can be superb. Research indicates that growing bags can be re-used with or without sterilization.	Watering and feeding are critical issues with high risk of poor quality or damaged fruit (black bottoms, blotch, etc.).
(4) Systems involving mineral rock wool, perlite, etc.	As above.	As above, but sterilization by heat highly practical.

Systems of Growing Tomatoes 23

Method of Growing	For	Against
(5) Hydroponics (N.F.T.)*	If approached scientifically with proper equipment, results can be excellent. It is claimed that N.F.T. is the system for the future.	This is not for the 'slap-dash' grower looking for something different or 'on the cheap'. Nutritional upsets can arise very rapidly and therefore fruit quality and yield can be variable.
(6) 'Hybrid' systems	Difficult to evaluate in view of the many variable issues involved. Properly performed ring culture can be superb but it tends to be used more for small-scale culture.	Apart from ring culture, properly executed, results can be extremely variable and not always entirely dependable.
(7) Straw bale or wad culture	A superb 'warm' start is ensured due to the heat generated by composting straw. Pest and disease free conditions are likely if clean straw is used.	Considerable quantities of water are required and bales are bulky although wads are less so. Nutritional upsets can occur due to varying nature of straw and its reaction to composting.
(8) Aeroponics	A controlled environmental system which promises well.	At this stage, 1982, it appears that the system is more suitable for warm climates.

*Nutrient Film Technique, see Chapter 15.

Chapter Three

The Propagation Stage of Tomatoes

Plant Raising

It is a modern view that plant raising in many spheres is best left in the hands of specialists and tomatoes are no exception. The contention is that standards of hygiene, consistency of plant material and the strict environmental control necessary are issues said to be taken more seriously by the specialist plant raiser than by the grower. It is also argued that it is cheaper at the end of the day to buy in plants. Against this it must be said that the tomato grower today must be a specialist anyway, so is able to raise plants of a high standard. The final decision must depend on the particular circumstances. The important thing is to ensure that good plants are available at the right time, as faulty plant material cannot be considered in view of the high investment involved in tomato production. So unless facilities for plant raising are good and the labour is available, it can be better to buy plants in.

Seed Sowing (See Composts, Chapter 17)

There are approximately 300 seeds per gram of average-sized tomato seed. Germination percentage should be high – around 80–90%. With the high price of hybrid seed today it is pointless to be wasteful, although it is useful to be able to select the best seedlings out of a batch. Standard size seed trays measure $14\frac{1}{2} \times 9 \times 2$ in (which is $36 \times 22 \times 5$ cm). It is usual to sow $\frac{3}{4}$ gram per tray (200 seeds). Compost for sowing can be all peat or peat/sand. Food content is not critical but physical condition is and whatever compost used must be free draining. Space sowing of tomatoes has never really been widely developed so far. This

26 The Propagation Stage of Tomatoes

involves setting the seed out in trays approximately 48 per tray or sowing directly into small pots, peat blocks or cell trays. There are growers who do this to advantage and if an acceptable system could be developed (see Lettuce, page 99) it is worth proceeding with. Trays are struck off level and the compost pressed down ½ in (12 mm) with a flat board before sowing the seed evenly by hand and covering lightly, *from a low level to avoid bringing the seeds to the surface.* Firming down is again advisable to try and keep seed coats below compost level, thus avoiding possible virus contamination between seedlings from the *outsides* of the seed coats.

Sowing for Grafting (See Page 35)
Either sow as above or, as is sometimes practised, space sow at 24 per seed tray. Note that the root stock is sown separately to the variety and approximately 2–14 days before it as germination of root stock seed tends to be slower. An alternative method is to sow one seed of the variety and one seed of the root stock about ¾ in (2 cm) apart in a 3½–4½ in (9–13 cm) peat or plastic pot to allow 'in situ' grafting. It is still advisable to phase sowing times (allowing a longer interval for early sowing, a shorter one for later sowing).

Germination
Tomato seeds germinate best in darkness so after sowing water with a fine rose to avoid uncovering the seed and stack the seed trays covered with polythene in batches, or alternatively cover the seed trays with black polythene or newspaper. The object in both instances is to conserve moisture. If germinating cabinets are available use these. The ideal temperature to aim at for germination for a variety of reasons, largely tied up with the physiology of the tomato, is 65°F (18°C) day and night, venting at 75°F (24°C) if necessary. Many growers section off a portion of their greenhouse with polythene and use a thermostatic electric fan heater to raise the temperature to the desirable level as this saves fuel. Should temperatures be higher during the germination period a greater percentage of non-productive or rogue 'male' plants could develop. These are short-jointed squat plants with an even true-leaf development. If temperatures during germination are lower, the 'breaking' of the seed can be patchy and uneven and bottom truss size and fruit setting can be adversely affected. Under the best conditions, seed will germinate between 6 and 8 days and, as soon as germination has occurred to a high percentage throughout the batch of seed, unstack or uncover and give full light treatment. Light treatment can then be given for three days at 15,000 lx on a 12–16 hour 'day'. Be careful *not* to allow drying out. On a large scale there is scope for a degree of mechanization for the whole process of seed sowing and germination, *including use of*

pelleted and 'bare' seed direct in peat or soil blocks. Research is also proceeding where seed or seedlings are placed direct in N.F.T. channels.

Potting and Compost

Within 10–12 days of sowing the majority of seedlings should be ready for potting (unless light treated). Views still differ on this due to the early truss initiation which takes place within the tomato seedling but in the absence of more definite information early pricking off when seed leaves are fully expanded is still advised. Large supplies of a selected suitably warmed compost must be conveniently on hand; so also must the necessary number of pots and containers being used. A wide range of compost can be used but in modern terms these are usually well textured and peat based (see Chapter 17), especially where peat culture systems follow as a 'feather' type of root system develops when growing plants in peat (see also Rock Wool). Some growers still prefer to use John Innes soil containing compost and for potting use the John Innes No. 1 (see Chapter 17). Once again texture of compost is a more important issue than nutrient status as plants will invariably be fed anyway while in their pots especially when they are in a peat-based compost. High nitrogen levels are not desirable at this stage and it will be found that peat-based compost tends to give a softer growth than soil-based types.

Pots

Size, shape and colour of pots for potting tomatoes is a matter which has undergone considerable investigation. For early crops the tendency is to use larger sized pots up to 5 in (12.5 cm) in diameter. Square pots can also be used and these have the advantage of fitting together and thus maximizing the use of space, particularly under lighting. It is a matter of choice whether plastic, paper, whale hide, polythene or peat pots are used. Soil blocks, or more accurately peat blocks, came back into popularity in the late 1970s, not only to avoid the high cost of pots, but to avoid planting checks, something which can be also achieved with a peat pot. Where the rock wool systems of culture are involved there is a range of rock wool cubes, each of which fit into each other. Another system used is plastic trays, or multipots and paper pots, especially for large-scale light treatment. Final selection of container must be on the grounds of personal experience or preference. A recent development is 'Firal' pots slotted at the base instead of having circular holes and these have become much more popular for hydroponic systems of culture as they allow better water uptake. The object of using larger pots especially for the early crop is to 'hold' the plants in them until 50% of the bottom flower truss is in bloom, or until the bottom truss is set. This acts as a 'brake' and is especially valuable during the poor light period early in the year. For later crops, size of pots is not so critical as plants usually get moved to their growing quarters more quickly and light levels are high enough to give balanced growth. Dark coloured pots are claimed to be 'warmer' than light coloured ones as they absorb solar heat more readily. Hygiene is essential for all pots, compost, benches, etc. and workers too should wear clean overalls and have clean hands.

Light Treatment
It is normal for early crops to be given artifical light treatment. There are various methods involved but the following basic information is broadly applicable. Plants are given 12–16 hours light treatment at 15,000 lx 24 for 10–21 days or longer. Temperatures should be in the order of 68°F (20°C) – 78°F (25°C) 'day' and 60°F (16°C) – 70°F (21°C) 'night'. Batch treatment is usual with lamps and sliding rails (also to allow ready watering), moving lights at 22.00 hours and 10.00 hours daily. White polythene is used to make the sides of a 'tent' and contain heat on benches.

Potting Procedures
There is need to evolve a handling procedure to minimize labour content for what is essentially a hand-performed operation, as there is little scope for automation due to the delicate nature of tomato seedlings. Ideally the work should be organized on a 'flow line' basis in a warm, comfortable place. Boxes of seedlings are brought in at one end to 'operators' who are provided with trays of pots filled with pre-warmed compost. Seedlings are teased out of the seed-boxes, held by their seed leaves and inserted into dibber holes made in the centre of each pot. Some selection of seedlings is important at this stage, avoiding those which are badly misshapen. Rogueing must be carried out slightly later, when true leaves have formed – discarding seedlings having the symmetrical true-leaf development, indicative of rogues or male plants. The trays containing the seedlings are tapped sharply on the bench and taken away to be replaced with another tray full of pots pre-filled with compost. Alternatively seedling boxes are taken by operators who are provided with piles of compost and supplies of pots. Pricking off may proceed as before with a dibber, or pots are half filled with compost, seedlings inserted in the centre and the pre-warmed compost eased around the seedlings with the fingers and firmed gently. In both cases finish with a sharp tap of the pot on the bench to firm it up. Great care is needed when potting seedlings in soil/peat blocks to avoid root breakage when filling up the block indent. Often it is better to merely drop them in and let seedlings develop their own roots rather than risk breakage. After the potting procedure, facilities must be available to

The Propagation Stage of Tomatoes

water lightly. Plants for grafting are pricked off into seed trays (unless space sown), filling the boxes with compost, striking level, inserting the seedlings 12–24 per tray and firming up before watering.

Capillary Benches

It can be useful to have a form of capillary bench watering, both under light treatment and for normal growing on of plants. Experience shows that under lights, soluble salts tend to be precipitated on the surface of both capillary matting and compost because of the heat generated by lights. Compost should have a low nutrient content for this procedure.

Chapter Four

Growing On Tomatoes

All available light, careful temperature control and, if necessary, plant foods, are the main criteria. Good light-admitting glasshouse structures are essential for winter propagation, properly sited to admit low-angled, winter sun. There must also be sensible placement of the plants within the structure whether on benches or on the floor. Evenly distributed warmth is also important, avoiding 'cold spots' and draughts. Temperatures for under light treatment aside, where standard greenhouse temperatures are involved, the aim should be to provide a *positive* day and *positive* night temperature (as registered on aspirated thermometers) related to the region concerned. There is still controversy in these matters. Generally speaking, higher *day* temperatures in the presence of good light tend to increase rate of growth and eventual fruit ripening but reduce the number of flowers in the lower trusses. Lower day temperatures may increase the number of flowers in the bottom truss but delay ripening. There may also be some effect on the ability of flowers to set and produce normal-sized fruits as opposed to 'chats'. Lowering the night temperature reduces the respiration of the plant, so conserving supplies of carbohydrates and proteins, and helps with flower setting. If night temperatures should be *too* low in relation to day temperatures, plants tend to have a surplus of carbohydrates and can become over-vigorous. The exact converse is true if the night temperatures are too high in relation to day temperatures. Should average temperatures be too low, day and night, and the plants subjected to a very chilly night in addition, plants tend to go hard and blue with considerable delay in fruting. The following *air* (ambient) temperatures

Growing On Tomatoes

are in general use for south and north of the U.K., stages 1, 2 and 3 applying to the propagation period.
1 Sowing to pricking out.
2 Pricking out to flower buds.
3 Before and after planting.
4 Later in season.

General Patterns of U.K. Temperatures

Stage	Night				Positive Day				Ventilation Commences At			
	'South'		'North'		'South'		'North'		'South'		'North'	
	°F	°C	°F	°C	°F	°C	°F	°C	°F	°C	°F	°C
1	65	18	65	18	65	18	65	18	74	24	74	24
2	60	16	56	13	64	18	64	18	74	24	74	24
3	62	17	56	13	68	20	68	20	74	24	74	24
4	62	17	56	13	64	18	64	18	68	21	68	20

Temperature patterns in Central Europe are broadly similar to 'South'.

Growing Temperatures (for plant raising and growing on)

Recent years and rising fuel prices have seen interest in soil or substrate/nutrient warming for fuel saving – by reducing *night* air temperatures to around 48–49°F (9°C), maintaining root zones at around 77°F (25°C). This is highly practical especially on N.F.T. and substrate (rock wool) systems. There has, however, been stem splitting, internode spacing and lowering of fruit quality.

Disease risk is also a hazard, especially in wet humid areas. Adopting low night temperatures *without* soil/substrate warming has, as one would expect, shown considerable loss in early yields – but as the season progresses yield reduction is less marked especially with plants grown later from the outset (Fairfield EHS Annual Report 1977).

One generally finds that some compromise in temperatures may be necessary as all growers do not have the same degree of sophistication for temperature control and ventilation, or for that matter soil warming facilities. A fair general target is around 56 to 58°F (14°C) night and 63–65°F (18°C) day with the proviso that the day temperature can be lowered a little during very dull weather. Ventilation should ideally take place at around 70–74°F (21–23°C). Recently, however, ventilation has been delayed to good effect to allow solar heat to 'bank' up. It is a wise procedure to have fairly accurate temperature recorders either with temperature bottles or at least a well-screened maximum and minimum thermometer. Thermostats should be aspirated.

Spacing Young Plants

As plants develop they will require more space. They must be spaced

Growing On Tomatoes

out on two or three occasions, ending up as wide apart as 12 × 12 in (30 × 30 cm). Failure to space out plants can result in them becoming spindly and drawn and the height of the bottom truss being raised considerably. There may even be a degree of 'missing' of the bottom truss. Many growers now 'space out' plants in their growing quarters during the pre-warming period prior to planting.

Watering Young Plants

The quantities of water needed by young plants depend on many factors. Peat or paper pots require less water than those of clay or plastic. They are best not kept too closely together as they may go soggy and disintegrate. Soil blocks, on the other hand, are best kept closely together and contained in trays or boxes. They must not be allowed to dry out as they can be extremely difficult to re-wet if they do. Compost type too may influence watering frequency, soil-based compost drying out more quickly than an all-peat mix. In the latter case take care to avoid over-watering as peat compost can look quite dry yet contain a lot of moisture. Plants on capillary watering systems are best in plastic pots with a rather gritty compost, otherwise the plants can quickly 'drown'. There can be no general rules for pot watering. Observation and adaptation to the circumstances must be the deciding criteria. Watering is best done by a slow running hose even on quite a large scale, although spray lines can be used with care until the foliage shrouds the pots. There is the problem, too, that the wet foliage will make the plants topple unless supported.

Feeding Young Plants

Whether or not young plants need feed depends again on pot size and compost type. Plants in large pots with John Innes compost could be perfectly happy but this is seldom so with soilless composts. Yellowing of lower leaves is the first indication that the plants are running out of food and by this time plants will almost certainly have suffered debility which will manifest itself at a later stage. Plants for the early crop will be around for quite a long while. So regular feeding is advisable on most counts as any possible detriment to subsequent performance is best avoided. Liquid feeding high in potash (see page 65) should be given at the correct dilution rate every 10–14 days with some plain water in between to avoid any possible salt build up. Later propagated plants which can develop in five weeks or less may not require any feeding. Here again it is best to err on the side of safety rather than have the plants going short of plant food. 24 oz per gallon potassium nitrate (150g/1 litre) diluted 1–200 is a 'normal' food, but there are many proprietary plant foods available to be used according to directions. These should also be high in potash.

34 Growing On Tomatoes

Support

Plants must at no stage be allowed to flop so this will mean support with split canes and the use of soft fillis if there is any risk of toppling. If support can be avoided it will save time and money.

Plant Raising Guide

Appearance	Possible Reason	Suggested Cure
Plants with long internodes, pale green leaves, although they have been fed and watered regularly.	Too little light and too high a temperature.	Decrease temperatures a little day and night.
Lower leaves yellowed with reduced colour and growth even with regular feeding.	Over-watering, excluding air from compost inhibiting the uptake of nutrient.	Less water plus 'safe' stimulant like dried blood at 2 oz/gal (12g/litre).
Dried and shrivelled leaf tips with spindly, stretched growth. Good colour.	Too much heat, probably during the day, due to lack of or insufficient ventilation.	Increase ventilation and damp down often; in hot weather, if unable to be continually present or with no automatic ventilation, leave vents open to be on the safe side during day.
Stocky, hard growth with lower leaves particularly coloured dark blue.	Too cold in greenhouse or perhaps affected by draughts.	Watch heating, especially at night, using max/min thermometer; check draughts with the addition of polythene curtains, particularly in the area of the doors.
Excessive curling with dark green leafed plants. Plants not growing quickly: leaf edges shrivelled, particularly growing tip.	Too much fertilizer or liquid feed application, which results in high salt concentration in the growing medium.	Give less fertilizer or liquid feed and give for a time plain water to flush out salt effect. (Soil analysis useful.)

Appearance	Possible Reason	Suggested Cure
Plants look pale or stunted and seed leaves dead.	One or other of the above. The condition of the seed leaves indicates well-being of the plant.	Growing conditions generally should be checked, using a liquid fertilizer diluted correctly.
Growth depression, mottling and 'blindness' of apical point.	Levels of fertilizer unbalanced or trace elements temporarily in short supply.	Feed concentration should be checked; minor irregularities usually correct themselves; weed–killer or chemical contamination could be a possibility and should not be dismissed.
General debility, distortion, wilting.	Virus/fungal disease and pest attack.	Pests and diseases; check symptoms, preventive and curative controls; generally checks to growth result in development of an excess of carbohydrates (causing 'soft' plants) which can readily be plundered by weak pathogens.

Carbon Dioxide (CO_2) Enrichment

It is standard practice and has proved beneficial in many nurseries to give three-fold enrichment with carbon dioxide to around 1,000 ppm (vpm). This supplements a natural complement of carbon dioxide gas in the atmosphere and accelerates the growth of plants, at the propagation and early growing-on stage. Special paraffin or propane burners are available, each specific to a given area. This applies to both propagating and early growing stages. CO_2 can be supplied from bulk tanks.

Grafting Tomatoes

The basic principles of grafting are well known and in the case of tomatoes it is a question of fully exploiting the vigour, pest and disease resistance of specially developed root stocks. This allows normal varieties to be grown in unsterilized soil when joined on to them by the

36 Growing On Tomatoes

process of grafting. Root stock seed is available in two forms: (1) K.V.F.N. (resistant to corky root, fusarium, nematodes and verticillium wilt (see Chapter 11 for details of pest and diseases); (2) Virus resistant forms of root stock, notably T.M.P.V.F.N. This overcomes one of the basic problems of grafting which is the spread of virus disease between root stock and variety and vice versa. It is an interesting fact that while certain resistances are now inbred into the modern varieties of 'straight' tomatoes, those marketed in Europe are invariably F1 hybrids. It nevertheless seems difficult to impart into these F1 varieties the degree of resistance necessary to overcome most troubles and yet still retain fruiting qualities. This is why the use of 'non-fruiting', highly resistant root stock still remains a practical proposition.

Organization for Grafting (See Figure 1)

Where seeds have been sown and pricked off into boxes, and batches of both are available as sturdy 4–6 in (10–15 cm) tall seedlings, they are then available for grafting. It is important not to have the plants too soft or floppy as this makes grafting more difficult. Ideally two

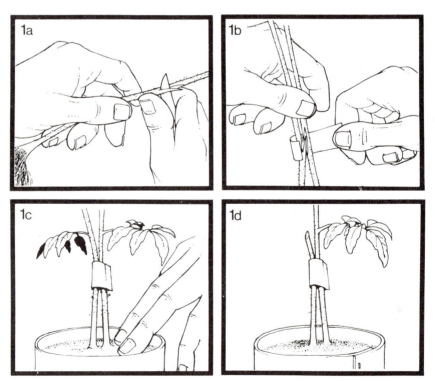

Figure 1 Grafting tomatoes is a technique which is certain to regain favour as it avoids the high costs of soil sterilization.

operators are required for grafting but it can be done by one person. One operator first takes the root stock plant and the other a variety plant, removing the seed leaves from both. This can be done 'en masse' before starting grafting to speed up the process. Wilting of the plants will quickly occur however unless they can be put into shallow trays of water. A downward cut with a scalpel or a clean one-sided razor blade is made in the root stock ½ in long (around 125 mm) without weakening the stem (Figure 1a) and a corresponding upward cut made in the variety. The two lips are then fitted together while another operator wraps 1 in (2.5 cm) wide transparent tape from a dispenser around the two stems at the cut area (Figure 1b). The plants are now carefully potted up into 3½ to 5 in (9–13 cm) pots and the *top* leaves of the root stock removed (Figure 1c). They can, if desired, be removed before grafting.

When direct sowing has been done in pots the general procedure is similar although it can be more difficult to operate, and breakages must be guarded against. The plants are in this case left in their pots undisturbed. A form of inarching is best – avoiding cuts.

After grafting the plants are put on benches and ideally polythene 'tents' or drapes are put over them supported by strings or wires to increase humidity and help union between the grafts. These polythene tents or drapes should not be left on longer than necessary and should be removed as soon as it is seen by inspection through the tape that the grafts have taken. Infection can easily be spread during the grafting process. This involves not only virus but other diseases, so it is advisable to dip the cutting blade frequently into a solution of 2% tri-sodium phosphate to kill off possible infection. Clean hands too are important. After grafting the plants may need feed as for 'normal' plants. Good light and spacing is also important. At planting time it is frequently recommended that if the variety root is left it can act as a carrier of vascular root and stem infection (Figure 1d). In practice it would seem that this does not readily occur as the variety root tends to wither away, or is not conductive of disease to any great extent.

The *top* of the root stock should be cleanly cut away *immediately above* the graft area at planting time but it will be found that re-growth will occur and must be continually removed during the season. The success of cultural systems such as bolsters place some doubt on the economic viability of the grafting technique as it is time consuming. If labour is available as it often is at that particular time, this is not a serious drawback. Grafted plants also tend to be over-vigorous and difficult to control, which can result in very large fruit.

Chapter Five

Planning for Planting Tomatoes

Growing crops for profit can be no hit-or-miss affair in these inflationary days. There is so much capital tied up in a crop that management decisions must be clear cut and carefully taken after consideration of all important factors. (In this respect, of course, tomatoes are no exception.) Whether it is a new block of glass or an older one, continuing in tomato crops or changing from other crops, there are many issues to be taken into account. Border-grown crops can only be satisfactory where previous crops have been of a high order indicated by yields, freedom from serious pests (mainly eelworm), diseases and other related matters. These are issues which can only be decided by strict observation and perusal of records. Soil analysis and eelworm counts are routine for all large-scale growing activities, and pathological reports relating to any crop failure are vital. When any doubts about the use of greenhouse borders begin to arise other cultural systems start to look attractive. Conversely the cost of alternative systems coupled with the type of watering and feeding equipment necessary cannot be lightly set aside. To face additional capital expenditure may not be possible.

Differences in Annual Cost of Three Systems of Growing a Long-term Tomato Crop

Fully accurate costing figures relating to different systems are not easily obtained and the following must only be taken as a guide on three major systems in 1978. Despite inflation since then they show comparative costs. (Information supplied by West of Scotland Agricultural College.)

40 Planning for Planting Tomatoes

Annual Cost (£/100m²)	Soil	Peat Bags	NFT
Plant raising	73.07	73.07	73.07
Fuel	413.12*	396.12*	304.69*
Electricity	39.61*	31.68*	23.76*
Peat Mulch	9.00	–	–
Water	5.07	3.34	2.46
Fertilizer	34.00	42.00	96.00
Growing Bags	–	82.08*	–
Polythene floor covering	–	6.41*	–
Channels – pumps	–	–	52.6
Irrigation	16.32	21.26	–
Capillary matting	–	–	13.30
Analysis	2.37	2.37	9.48
Solution heating	–	–	3.10
Packaging at 21.5 p/unit	88.79*	104.49*	104.49*
TOTAL	681.35	762.82	684.96

*Has risen considerably in 1982.

In situations where there is little or no good soil on site decisions are made easier.

Standard Labour Use

Standard labour costs vary somewhat and here are some comparative figures relating to different methods.

Job	Total time allowed (hr/100m²)		
	Soil	Peat	NFT
1 Preparation of house	22.6	8.1	6.0
2 Propagation of plants	6.6	6.6	6.0
3 Growing on of plants	3.5	3.7	3.0
4 Training and layering	46.8	47.5	47.5
5 Watering and feeding	5.0	4.5	3.0
6 Harvesting	30.0	34.4	34.4
7 Clearing crop	5.3	2.8	2.0
TOTAL	119.8	197.5	107.9

N.F.T. Capital Investment Appraisal

Trough system	*Cost £/100m²	Life (yrs)	Annual Cost (£/yr/100m²)
1 Formed concrete	526	10	52.6
2 Metal staging Poly trough**	431	10	65.6
3 Concrete floor Poly trough**	491	10	71.6
4 Poly Trough** Insulation*** (Double planting system)	185	1–2	99.5
5 Poly trough** Insulation**	371	1–2	199.5

*Cost – includes plumbing, pumps, etc. and is assumed to have a life of 10 years.
** 1 year life
*** 2 year life
See Chapter 15 for discussions on N.F.T.

Planning for Planting Tomatoes

Annual Cost (£/100m²)	Soil	Peat Bags	NFT

Total Annual Cost – Labour and Materials (£/100m²)

	Soil	Peat	NFT
Material	681.29	762.82	685.40
Labour at £1.50 hr	179.70	161.25	152.85
TOTAL	860.99	924.07	838.25

Annual Net Margin (See Also Chapter 10)

Revenue (£0.51/kg) £/100m²	1053.81	1239.75	1239.75
Less Annual Cost £/100m²	860.99	924.07	838.25
Annual Net Margin	192.82	315.68	401.50

Selection Table Under Glass or Plastic

Crop performance (if previous crop grown)	Root condition	Light and heat levels	Ventilation, watering and feeding facilities	Decisions
Good soil/new or sterilized. Good previous crop.	Good (white and not extensively diseased)	Good	Good	Border culture for all crops is practical – but consider other systems for maximizing yields.
Good soil. Previous crop – fairly good sterilization was performed as a routine matter.	Fair only	Fair	Fair	Only attempt a mid-season crop. Sterilization essential as an insurance.
Soil bad – which has resulted in poor crop. Soil sterilization not considered practical.	Very poor	Good	Fair to Good	Do not grow in borders, selecting an alternative method. On a limited scale consider grafted plants.
Soil good – and previous crops reasonable but sterilization not possible for various reasons.	Fair	Bad	Fair	Mid-season or later crops only. Use grafted plants or go on to alternative method.
Soil poor. Results poor or crop a failure.	Very bad	Very poor	Bad	Only attempt a later 'follow-on' crop using a container or module system.

Having decided either on economic or cultural grounds what method to adopt, it is then a case of planning a work programme.

Chapter Six

Border Cultivation of Tomatoes

The important issues in border cultivation are drainage, soil depth and evenness of distribution, especially if site levelling has taken place prior to glasshouse erection. A few inspection holes will not go amiss and the same holes can be used to check drainage. This not only ascertains sub-soil type and condition, but finds out how quickly, if at all, water put into an inspection hole with a hose drains away. Should drainage be shown to be bad then tile/plastic pipes should be installed at a depth and distance apart appropriate to soil type. Seepage from surrounding and especially higher land should be taken into account and steps taken to trap the moisture in a catchment drain, *outside* the glasshouse or structure.

Important Note:
In areas of poor or no soil – or soil such as in the Mediterranean zones – elaborate special preparations may be necessary involving layers of manure or compost or of course alternative systems. These notes therefore apply to U.K. culture systems in soil.

Soil Analysis and Adjustment of Nutrient Levels
(See Also Chapter 15, N.F.T. and Rock Wool Systems)

This is an essential prerequisite to any cropping programme where border soils are involved. (It is also useful for potting media.) For other cropping systems such as grow bags, analysis is also routine, but this is usually performed during the growing season. Soil analysis is performed by either commercial or advisory service laboratories in most developed countries. Charges for this service vary and may even be free for large-scale customers of chemical firms. Many large growers have facilities for limited aspects of analysis, usually pH (soil acidity or alkalinity) and soluble salts.

44 Border Cultivation of Tomatoes

pH
This should be between 6 and 6.5 for soil or between 5.5 and 6 for a peat-based soilless media (e.g. grow bags, etc.) A lime requirement figure is usually given with the analysis. Where self-performed pH analysis with indicator fluid or pH meter is involved, it is a question of trial and error as soils vary a great deal in type and react differently to lime quantities. On average 6–8 oz per sq yd (203–271 g/m^2) is a normal dressing to adjust the pH but it is impossible to state exactly the lime requirement without a figure calculated by the analyst.

Nitrogen**
This is a figure which varies widely, according to season and whether the soil has been heat sterilized or not. The addition of farmyard manure (FYM) also influences nitrogen levels considerably. Nitrogen levels are determined in ppm (parts per million/ mg/litre) nitrate and levels of between 51–100 ppm (mg/litre) are generally considered optimal for tomatoes. This corresponds to index 2, above which figure no nitrogen should be added in base feeds. As a general rule, following heat sterilization, complete base feeds *low* or zero in nitrogen are applied. Where 'straight' fertilizers are preferred in most types of soils, ¾ oz per sq yd of ammonium nitrate (25 g/m^2) = ¼ oz to ⅓ oz sq yd (7–9 g/m^2) of *actual* nitrogen, will result in an index change of one digit (approximately).

Phosphorus**
This is determined in mg/100 g P$_2$O$_5$ or ppm (mg/litre). P standards are 50–60 mg/100 g P$_2$O$_5$ 71–140 ppm (mg/litre) P (sodium bicarbonate extraction). This corresponds to index 5–6, above which figure no phosphorus addition is necessary. The addition of ¾ oz per sq yd of triple superphosphates (47% P$_2$O$_5$) (25 g/m^2) (= ½ oz per sq yd (12 g/ m^2) of *actual* phosphoric acid) will result in an index change of approximately 1 digit.

Potassium**
This is generally reported in ppm (mg/litre) K in soil on ammonium nitrate extract 0–3, 600 (index 0–9) or ammonium acetate/acetic acid extract 0–3,000 (index 0–9).

Index 4–5 (405–900 ppm K and 355–700 ppm K) is standard for most greenhouse crops. It can also be reported in mg/100 g K$_2$O and stated as low, medium or high. (Adding 3 oz of sulphate of potash per sq yd (100 g^2) = 1½ oz per sq yd of *actual* potash (50 g^2) will result in an index change of approximately 1 digit.

Magnesium**

Reported generally on ammonium nitrate extract as ppm (mg/litre) mg in soil the scale is 0–1500 (index 0–9). Indexes in the 3–5 range are normal but ratio of magnesium to potassium is important. Calcium to magnesium rate 10/1 is critical with tomatoes to avoid blossom end rot. The addition of 3 oz of Keizerite (17% mg) (100 g/m^2) approx ¾ oz (24 g/m^2) of actual magnesium will result in an index change of approximately 1 digit.

Soluble Salts pC (Potential Coefficient)

This is a measure of soil conductivity and important for tomatoes to control vigour of growth. ADAS do this on the saturated calcium sulphate technique ranging from 1900–4000 mhos (microsiemens) (index 0–8). Indices around 3–4 are usual. Other laboratories and growers with meters calculate on pC scales, safe levels being 2.8–3.00. Other methods are in use, such as conductivity factors (CF).

The comparison is as follows:

ADAS SCALES Index 3–4 (2610–2800) (mhos microsiemens) = CF 16–10 = pC 2.8–3.00

**Important Note:*
Figures will vary according to analysis procedures and these are 'standards' to ADAS Scales. (See MAFF Booklet G.F.I. Fertilizer Recommendations for Agricultural and Horticultural Crops.)

Balance of Main Nutrients

What is often more important than actual quantities available is the balance of the main nutrients to each other, especially in the case of tomatoes with the balance of nitrogen to potash which should be broadly in the ratio of 1 nitrogen to 3 potassium.

Tissue Analysis

This is a task primarily for the well-equipped laboratory. Discs are now available for a quick determination of leaf nutrient content.

Organic Matter

This is a very useful figure to have prior to border culture and can be provided by the soil analyst if asked for. (It is also a useful figure for potting composts.) Soils with a high organic matter are usually of good physical structure. Figures vary according to 'with' or 'without' moisture but between 10–12% (including moisture) is normal. A higher figure up to 15% (including moisture) is preferable but low figures are by no means diastrous to the crop; in certain areas of Holland and the Middle East tomatoes are grown in almost pure sand. This may also be said of many regions in southern Spain, especially Almeria where plastic structures are erected on coastal strips of sandy soil and it is only possible to grow the crop well by spreading a mulch of organic matter on top of the sand. Whether farmyard manure, peat or other organic material is added to the soil depends not only on analysis figures but the 'feel' of the soil. This is related not only to moisture-holding content of the soil but the way in which the soil may 'pan' on water application. This means quite simply that the top soil 'caps' and the moisture runs over the surface instead of penetrating down through it to where the plant roots are. Note that where farmyard manure (FYM) is added this contains nutrients and will reduce the total need for base dressings. This is especially important with regard to the nitrogen content, particularly where sterilization by heat is involved. It can be almost impossible to control the growth of plants in borders which are steamed following heavy application of farmyard manure (FYM). (Normal rate of FYM dressing is around 25–30 tons per acre (62–75 tonnes/ha).) *Peat is a much 'safer' form of organic matter to use* at around 10 tons/acre/25 tonnes/ha.

Soil Sterilization (See Chapter 16)
Where sterilization has to be carried out this must be arranged in between crops at some convenient time. This is usually as soon as the previous crop has been removed and the greenhouse fumigated and/or washed down. Sheet steaming is frequently carried out for tomato borders to reduce labour. Old-fashioned grid steaming, working entirely by hand, is still practised by smaller growers but, on a larger scale, grid steaming is carried out by a movable winch. Alternatively, chemical sterilization by means of Basamid (Dazomet) or Methyl Bromide is an effective labour-saving alternative. Note that Methyl Bromide should be contractor applied (restrictions to use possibly pending).

Flooding
Whether or not it is necessary to pre-water border soil will depend principally on the level of soluble salts and this can only be determined by analysis. Where soluble salts are shown to be dangerously high, figures *below* pC 2.8 – 3 (CF16–10) or much *above* index 4, then flooding would be advisable (seek advice from an expert in this instance, see also p. 45). This is best carried out with mist spray lines to avoid soil structure damage. The quantity of water required will vary according to soil type but is generally in the order of 20,000 – 40,000 gallons per acre (288,000 – 500,000 litres/ha) for light and heavy soils respectively.

Chapter Seven

Preparation of Borders for Tomatoes

Cultivation is an important issue, either by digging on a small scale, ploughing or rotary cultivating. There are various machines which will carry out digging mechanically. Incorporating organic matter (if this is indicated by analysis or other considerations) is usual at the cultivation stage using FYM or peat. Methods of achieving this to avoid high labour depend on the equipment available and, while it is possible to use manure spreaders on a large scale, considerable glass-fouling is likely with FYM so that hand shovelling from a trailer is more likely to be practical. After cultivation the soil is allowed to dry out before levelling and raking and finally applying base fertilizers if needed. These are applied evenly either by spreader or by hand and lightly rotovated in to 5–6 in (12–15 cm) depth only. This is preferably done approximately 6–8 days before planting, leaving the soil firm, moist and sufficiently warm.

Application of Base Feeds
The nutrient needs of a 60–100 ton crop per acre (150–200 tonnes/ha) are in the order of:
1,000 – 1,600 lb potash (454–726 kg)
 500 –   800 lb nitrogen (227–363 kg)
 100 –   150 lb phosphorus (45–68 kg)
 130 –   220 lb magnesium (59–99 kg)
 600 – 1,000 lb calcium (272–454 kg)
Allowing for a 15–20% drainage loss and fixation of phosphate, about 50% of the nitrogen/potash/magnesium and calcium applied is considered available to the plants and about 20% of the phosphorus.

Preparation of Borders for Tomatoes

Although the figures could vary greatly according to cultural method, the general situation is as follows:

	Plant Needs
Base fertilizer application	¼ – ⅓ of total
Plus reserves in soil	⅓ up to ½ of total
Plus liquid feeding or top dressings	To make up total crop needs and this will vary according to length of season and total yield

Note with the high yields now being achieved, and especially with container or other systems, there is much more dependence on seasonal feeding. (In the case of hydroponic systems, *total* dependence is the case.) It can be dangerous to attempt to supply more than ⅓ to ½ of the nutrient needs at the outset owing to problems of soluble salt damage. It is a question of constant scrutiny of the crop, analysis and modification according to needs, a matter discussed later under seasonal feeding.

Base Feed Applications

Type of crop	Soil treatment	Base fertilizer type	Quantity per sq yard
Early and main crop tomatoes	Sterilized by heat	*High potash base	6 oz (203 g/m^2)
		Sulphate of potash	2–3 oz (68–101 g/m^2)
		Magnesium sulphate	2–3 oz (68–101 g/m^2)
Early and main	Chemically sterilized or unsterilized	*Medium (standard) potash base	6 oz (203 g/m^2)
		Magnesium sulphate	3 oz (101 g/m^2)
Late tomatoes (heated or cold grown)		*High potash base	6 oz (203 g/m^2)
		Magnesium sulphate	3 oz (101 g/m^2)
Late tomatoes (heated or cold grown)		Medium potash base	6 oz (203 g/m^2)
		Magnesium sulphate	3 oz (101 g/m^2)

*Or straight fertilizers to index factors (see page 44).

Preparation of Borders for Tomatoes 49

Magnesium sulphate is not generally applied if there is a high soluble salt content and flooding has *not* been carried out for various reasons. Modification of base feeds may be necessary according to whether vigorous or weak varieties are grown. Soil analysis will of course also confirm the amount of base needed if any. When tomatoes follow a lettuce crop it is usual to give a higher nitrogen type of fertilizer to replace the nitrogen taken up by the lettuce, but analysis will confirm this.

Typical Tomato Base Fertilizer Analysis (Proprietary)

Base fertilizer	Nitrogen % N	Phosphorus % P_2O_5		Potash % K_2O
		Sol.	Insol.	
'Standard'	9.5	9	0.5	13.2
'High potash'	6	10	0.5	17.5
'High nitrogen' (seldom necessary)	12	5.5	0.5	6
John Innes base (use as high potash)	5.2	7	0.5	10

Plant Spacing

Density of plants can vary per acre from around 11,000 up to 15,000 or 16,000 with 12,000 or 13,000 being normal. A lot will depend on variety, vigorous varieties being given more room than weak growers (see Figure 2), and region. The problem is with so many new varieties it is difficult to know what their vigour group is. The most usually accepted norm is 5 ft (1.5 m) double rows and heating loops are generally run at this distance apart to correspond. Where warm water systems are involved it is usual to put two rows of plants one on each side of the heating pipes 18 in (46 cm) apart – the plants 11–15 in (26–38 cm) apart in the row. Four rows (2 double rows) fit in well with the Venlo type of greenhouse which has 10 ft 6 in (3.2 m) single spans. It is also suitable for the 21 ft (6.4 m) double spans (four double rows) and the standard 22 ft (6.7 m) structures.

'Timetable' for Border Planting Systems

When grafted plants are involved, the treatment outlined is basically similar. The difference is that sterilization either by heat or chemicals is generally *not* necessary unless of course there is a serious disease or weed problem, the latter likely to be the case when new glasshouses are erected on a new site. (Basamid can generally deal with these.)

50 Preparation of Borders for Tomatoes

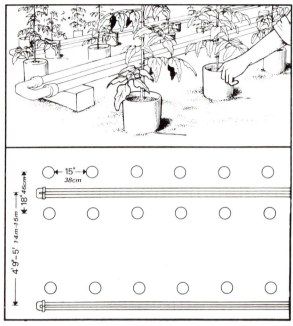

Figure 2 Spacing plants depends much on arrangement of heating pipes, width and height of greenhouse or structure and other considerations. This spacing is generally acceptable.

1. An assessment of previous performance of crop and rooting systems examination to ascertain best way of dealing with the next crop, plus the necessary sterilization. — Oct-Nov. Chemically sterilize with Metham-sodium (See Chapter 16 for further details on sterilization).

2. Soil analysis and eelworm count – particularly check soluble salt level. — November

3. Weed removal (grafted plants), subsoil loosening and cultivation generally. — December

4. The incorporation of organic matter such as FYM, peat, etc. complements cultivation. — December

5. Flooding if advisable. — December-March

6. Apply lime if necessary, taking into account pH and lime requirement figure. — January-March

7. If borders are too dry, pre-planting watering. — January-March

Preparation of Borders for Tomatoes

8 6–8 days before planting, apply base   January–May
dressings (not a vital issue). Turn on heat
to warm soil.
9 Rake and fork soil reasonably level.   January–May

Preparation for Modular Systems
'Grow Bags' or Peat Modules (Bolsters)

Sterilization of soil is not required. The whole greenhouse area is levelled and covered with black/white polythene, white up, and this will act not only as a barrier to weeds and pest and disease but help with light reflection which is particularly useful early in the season. Before the bolsters are spaced out it must be decided what pattern of planting is to be followed and what density of plants is suitable. This is a matter also discussed for border grown crops.

Following the double row system the bolsters are laid in a double row at 5 ft (1.5 m) centres. Where capillary matting is to be used under the bolsters or bags it is necessary to make depressions 2 or 3 in deep (5 to 7.5 cm) and lay the capillary matting on this. The bolsters are well pierced underneath with a fork, before being put down on top of the matting. It is not necessary to spread polythene over the whole house area and strips may be perfectly satisfactory. Whether to run rows North/South or East/West is also a matter for planning, the former being general. Experimental work with double cropping of grow bags placed in position has taken place at a number of centres. There are many different permutations, but all basically involve laying down the grow bags in a double row as described and planting either 6 plants per bag for each crop, or 3 per bag for first crop, followed by 3 per same bag for second crop (see Figure 3).

Plants were taken to 9–10 trusses on first crop – and heavily deleafed to allow development of second crop. Crop yields and labour savings over conventional growing do not show double cropping to great advantage on these systems. There is also some evidence to show that grow bags can be used a second time with or without sterilization. While this shows savings in capital expenditure whether it is practical depends on crop timing.

Rock Wool Systems

The layout is broadly similar to bolsters, rock wool blocks being laid end to end or in 'blocks'. Isolation from the border with polythene is essential. Another feature of rock wool culture is the need to put down some form of insulation below the rock wool to avoid the heat going downwards into the border from heating pipes or soil-warming cables if installed on top of the rock wool, although there tends to be some

52 Preparation of Borders for Tomatoes

conflict of view whether this is advantageous or otherwise. (Details of setting up the system are given in Chapter 15.)

The same basic timing will apply but there will be no flooding, base application or treatment of border generally.

Figure 3 Bolsters or grow bags for double cropping can be arranged on several permutations aimed at minimum output of labour and maximum yields.

Preparation of Borders for Tomatoes

N.F.T. and Other Systems

It is important to decide on planting dates and work backwards from these. The 'mechanics' of N.F.T. systems may take some time to organize but can be done anytime. (Details of N.F.T. for tomatoes and other crops are given in Chapter 15.)

Preparation for Straw Bales

This is a system which can give superb results where soils are pest infected or diseased and sterilization is considered impractical on economic grounds or otherwise. There are great benefits in using straw because of the heat generated when it is decomposing and also carbon dioxide gas which enriches the atmosphere. On the other hand the bales are bulky which means taking up valuable space. They are also heavy although effective mechanization can do a lot to reduce the labour load. The 5 ft (1.5 m) norm system is invariably followed and generally speaking complete bales are laid on their side in a polythene-lined depression to act as a barrier from pests and diseases, in a double row. Wads of straw 8 in (20 cm) thick can also be used and these are better put together to form a 2–3 wad width bed in a polythene 'trough'. The whole success of straw bale culture lies in getting the bales to break down rapidly and generate heat. It is important to try and find wheat straw which is slower to decompose and retains its shape better and, while old straw can be used, fresh bales are better. Get bales which have not been treated with the weed-killers TBA or Picloram as this will persist and result in considerable damage to the crop. Process of composting depends on the addition of chemicals. The first thing to ensure is that the greenhouse atmosphere is warm enough, which may necessitate putting on the heating system to bring the temperature over 50°F (10°C). The bales are thoroughly soaked with water, preferably with spray lines. For each cwt (50 kg) of dry straw (approx. 2 bales) it is normal to use 12 oz/350g of ammonium nitrate-lime (Nitro chalk 26% or similar), 12 oz (350 g) triple superphosphates, 8 oz (225 g) magnesium sulphate, 12 oz (350 g) potassium nitrate and 6 oz (170 g) ferrous sulphate. (This has been found beneficial in many cases.) This total amount of fertilizer, around 3 lb (1.3 kg), can be added in small quantities over a period of 9–12 days flushing in on each application. Much more simply, results can be almost as effective by using around 3 lb (1.3 kg) of a high nitrogen compound fertilizer *complete with trace elements* at the initial application, adding around 1 lb (450 g) of ammonium nitrate lime in around 9 days if the bales do not heat properly. Another method is to use a high nitrogen liquid fertilizer applied through the spray lines as this can be highly effective and, in addition to saving a lot of labour, it can avoid local fertilizers scorching which can occur when dry fertilizers are used, as 'flushing in' is never fully

Preparation of Borders for Tomatoes

effective. Fertilizers are used pro-rata for wads. The straw will heat up fairly rapidly until it reaches a temperature of 110 to 130°F (43–54°C). When the temperature drops to 90°F (32°C) a shallow ridge of peaty compost is run along the top of the bales and planting can take place provided the bales are still not too hot. It is usual to put about 3 plants per bale. Where wads are used, instead of a ridge of peaty compost, it is normal to use an even 2 in (5 cm) layer over the top of the wads, and space plants normally.

Preparations for Other Systems
These will vary considerably and, where ring culture is involved, a 5–6 in (12.5–15 cm) layer of weathered ash or other clean material is put over the top of the border. It is important that these ashes are *not* fresh, as, if so, they would likely contain sulphur. Bitumized paper 'rings' 9–10 in (25 cm) with or without bottoms are then spaced out at the decided distance. Quite often bitumized paper pots with bottoms are used and the plants housed together in a warm greenhouse before being set out in the growing greenhouse, to save fuel.

Chapter Eight

Planting of Tomatoes

Whatever system of culture is involved the planting of tomatoes should never take place until the border soil or growing medium is suitably warm and it is considered that the minimum temperature should be 56–57°F (14°C). This is *not* the surface temperature, but that at 4–5 in depth (10–12.5 cm), preferably taken *early* in the morning. With soil pipes placed adjacent to plant rows whatever system is involved, pre-warming is a lot easier, but where warm air heating is used, soil warming can take some considerable time. There has been in recent years considerable interest in the use of plastic pipes, connected to the heating system, buried in the soil 10–12 in (25–30 cm) below the plant rows and this can certainly raise the soil temperature very quickly. (Heating is stated as an inbuilt requisite with rock wool and N.F.T. systems, see Chapter 15.) Plants for the early crop can often be up to 2 ft (60 cm) tall (or more) but an ideal height would be around 12–14 in (30–35 cm) with, in the case of the early crop, the first truss of flowers fully developed and showing 50% colour. Various techniques for getting the plants into the growing medium are followed. Holes in greenhouse borders may be taken out in advance of planting with planting tools or trowels, to allow the soil at the base and sides to reach an acceptable temperature. Plants in soil blocks on the other hand are often left lying on the soil surface to root in as they wish and root out according to the soil temperature. Plants in plastic pots should be removed carefully without great disturbance while plants in paper or peat pots are planted without removal. Plants on N.F.T. systems are simply spaced out in the channels. Where bolsters or grow bags are concerned, it is usual to place the plants on top of the grow bags for a few days, before cutting circles or squares out, and setting in the plants with a trowel or planting tool. With 'rock wool' systems, plants are put on *top* of slabs in their

56 Planting of Tomatoes

'pots'. Depth of actual planting on any system is not a critical issue but seed leaves should be above the soil or growing medium surface.

Environmental Control and Flower Setting

'Setting' flowers is an essential part of tomato growing. Spraying with water and shutting the vents to raise humidity will assist pollen to fall on to the stigma and germinate. This should be done *only* on sunny days for an hour or so in the morning. Electric vibrators (Electric 'Bees') will also help with setting, especially early in the year and spraying with *droplets* of water (sprinklers) is also helpful. Flower setting is of course also related to pollen viability – which is linked to variety, light levels and the vigour of plants – and it is essential *not* to allow plants to get into over vigorous growth patterns – due to excess nitrogen, high day/low night temperatures.

Letting the plants show 50% flower before planting is thought essential for early plantings – and feed strength must be kept at suggested levels to control growth by 'osmosis' when the plants' uptake of moisture is limited by the nutrient concentration in the growing medium (see page 64).

Early Treatment – Summary

Cultural method	Early waterings	State of growing medium	Environmental control
Border, which includes grafted plants	Only sufficient watering in the area of root ball to prevent wilting in the first week or so.	Apply moisture overall by spray line.	High humidity desirable with limited ventilation until plants show signs of growing as indicated by freshening of the growing tips. Frequent damping.
Straw bales	Make sure plants do not dry out as they frequently can, due to the heat of the bales or wads.	Keep bales or wads moist with spray line.	Because of the amount of moisture on the bales or wads the atmosphere is usually moist enough.
Bolsters or grow bags	The very minimum of water in the root area preferably by hand.	Peat-based growing media usually stay sufficiently moist provided they are well watered at the outset, but definitely not to the saturation point.	As for border plants. Some damping to raise humidity.

Planting of Tomatoes

Cultural method	Early waterings	State of growing medium	Environmental control
N.F.T.	The plants are adequately supplied with moisture.	The important issue is that the water flow is correct, the slope sufficient so that the roots are not 'drowned'. Intermittent flow may be desirable.	As for border plants – but with little damping unless for flower setting.
Container systems	Where soil is involved as with ring culture, etc. treat as for border grown plants. Where soilless composts are being used, treatment should be similar to that for grow bags or bolsters.	Where large amounts of soil are involved, no further large-scale watering is generally required till the plants start to grow strongly.	Damping down by mist sprays of the whole greenhouse is the rule.

Chapter Nine

Plant Training of Tomatoes

Recent years have seen considerable modifications in training systems, aimed not only at avoiding the high labour content of working with plants when they reach a certain height, but to boost crops to an almost unprecedented level by lateral training systems enabling stem elongation to go on well into the autumn. Much will of course depend on the nature of the crop. If it is a short-term one or double cropping is intended, it will be a case of taking the plants up to the height of the horizontal wires and perhaps a little beyond. The wires spread across the house or structure at gutter height are the mainstay of all training systems and it is essential that these wires be strong enough and the house be braced to take the weight of the fully laden tomato crop. This is a matter to discuss with the glasshouse or structure designer. Instances where the ends of sides of a greenhouse have been pulled down by crop weight are not unknown. With the short-term or double crop, 3–5 ply fillis or polypropylene twine is tied in a loose knot around the lowest leaves of the plant and secured straight up to the horizontal wires, being tied there with a bow knot for easy removal or for dropping the plants slightly should this be necessary. Plant wires or hooks are also used to avoid root 'pulling' (see Figure 5a) on non-border systems. Alternatively, plants, when they reach the top of the string, can be trained at an angle towards the roof of the structure. This method is seldom used now for long-term crops.

Fairfield Layering System
This method, developed at the Fairfield Experimental Station, Lancashire, and used by a number of growers in this region and elsewhere, involves taking the plants up to the wire, loosening the string, and if long enough, retying it at approximately 3 ft (1 m) further along the

60 Plant Training of Tomatoes

wire. This is a continual process, being repeated each time the growing point of the plant reaches the wire so it involves a fair amount of labour. It may be necessary to add to the length of the string which also takes time. Another method is to use a series of S-hooks set 14–15 in apart at plant spacings and made of 16-gauge galvanized wire. When the plants are initially tied up, sufficient string is used so that the plants may be gradually dropped so many hooks along as they develop (Figure 5b). Ideally with these layering systems, it is unsatisfactory to put the fillis or twine round the bottom of the plant. It is better supported to horizontal wires secured to wooden stobs and this also prevents the bottom trusses from trailing on the growing medium. (A further modification is the 'coathanger' system, or rotary wheel, Flymco, method where all the spare twine is wrapped around a coathanger or holder, see Figure 4.)

Modified Guernsey Method

This is ideal for high guttered structures. In addition to the normal vertical wires above each plant row an arch of wires is provided generally over the path area so that the plants can be run across in an archway. A considerable amount of work is necessary to train the new growth in and keep the head pointing upwards to receive sufficient light. Breakage can readily occur too (see Figure 5c).

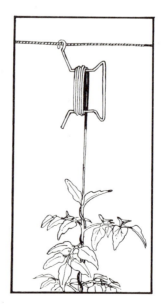

Figure 4 'Coathangers' are useful for holding spare twine on layering systems.

Plant Training of Tomatoes 61

Cordon Method
In this method vertical strings are used and the plants initially taken up to them but as the plants develop they are run at an angle to additional string run diagonally across the vertical strings. Provided this method is done correctly it spaces the plants out and has many advantages, provided the crop is adequately de-leafed (see Figure 5d). The development of a training method must depend on the precise

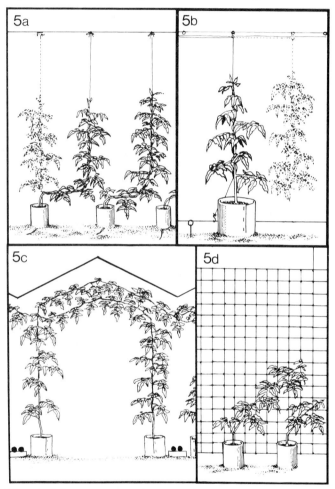

Figure 5 Plant training systems take many forms:
5a Plants taken up to wire and then layered by undoing and re-tying twine
5b As (5a) but using S hooks (or 'coathangers')
5c Arch systems
5d Layering from outset on vertical and horizontal twine or nets (nets used on Continent)

62 Plant Training of Tomatoes

circumstances. The respective labour involvement in the various methods differs. Efford E.H.S. are evaluating different systems including double cropping but results are somewhat inconclusive.

In an effort to reduce labour, 'automatic' layering systems are being developed – based on a moving wire support. To be successful overhead wires must be directly above plants to avoid 'hang out'.

Plant Pruning

This is an essential part of tomato culture. It involves removing side shoots which form in the axils of the leaves and may also develop at ground level, particularly with plants on root stocks. A proportion of the upper leaves are also removed, especially when plants are on the layering system. Obviously leaves should not be needlessly removed until they have served their purpose. During the early part of the season it is usual to remove leaves up to the ripening truss, but as the season progresses, modern practice is to leave only 3–4 ft (1 m) at the top of the plant with its leaves. A proportion of remaining leaves are also removed to avoid congestion. Leaves snap off easily if the plant is full of moisture which is usually early in the morning. Leafing, as it is called, must be done on a definite work programme system, otherwise plants could quickly get out of hand, to the detriment of the crop, and more importantly circulation of air could be hindered and disease encouraged. Provided environmental control is good, the scars left following de-leafing will generally heal, but if there is any doubt, it is advisable to go on to a regular *botrytis* (grey mould) prevention programme (see page 72).

Watering and Feeding

Quantities of water used by tomato plants are very considerable and it is necessary to determine precisely how much water the crop requires. On a small scale, moisture meters can be used and these are even useful for the larger grower, provided sufficient of them are available to give an overall picture. Instruments called Evaporimeters, including 'automatic' types, are really quite simple bits of apparatus which if used according to directions ensure an accurate water supply for the plants. Much more sophisticated equipment is available, operating by light input. As a complete alternative to these methods, there is a fairly accurate, widely used water requirement table based on the weather pattern.

Plant Training of Tomatoes

Approximate Water Requirement Per Day
Calculated at a planting density of 3 plants/m² (12,000 plants/acre), and plants over 3 ft or 1 m high (U.K.)

Weather Pattern	Litre/m²	(gal/acre)	Litre/plant	(pint/plant)
Very dull/cloudy and dull most of the day	0.66	600	0.14–0.28	¼–½
Dull/overcast most of the day	1.1	1,000	0.28–0.42	½–¾
Fairly sunny/cloudy with bright periods	2.75	2,500	0.71–0.85	1¼–1½
Sunny/only occasional cloud	3.85	3,500	1.1–1.2	2–2¼
Very sunny/sky clear and sunny all day	5.5	5,000	1.5–1.8	2¾–3¼

Modification will of course be required for the cultural method involved as some systems 'lose' more water than others through drainage and evaporation. It is necessary to have a watering system where the quantity of water applied is known. The most normal methods of watering large-scale tomato growing units are trickle systems but spray lines can also be used, low and high level or both. Watering needs for border-grown plants can be reduced to a certain extent by mulching with straw or peat. At the end of the day, visual assessment will tell whether the plants are being well enough supplied with water. Water-logged plants tend to grow lighter in colour accompanied by yellowing of the bottom leaves. Under-watered plants will not only wilt in hot sun but can go a dark green colour and the foliage becomes hard. The margins of the leaves especially near the growing point of the plant can often become scorched too. More important it will be found that the setting of the flowers is bad with flower dropping too and there can be blossom end rot (Black Bottoms). Whatever method of water application is decided upon its labour content should be low. There are electronic methods of applying water and plant foods, which are worth investment on a large scale.

Feeding (See N.F.T., Rock Wool Sections)
Not so many years back there was considerable argument as to whether tomato plants growing in a well-prepared greenhouse border required regular feeding or not. Modern views however, almost universally, adopt the principle that for maximum yields plants must be constantly fed no

64 Plant Training of Tomatoes

matter what method of culture is involved. Regular analysis is the rule. See page 44 for standards at which to aim.

The whole basis of feeding tomato plants is on the principle of high potash to nitrogen ratios (3/1) to begin with. It is normal in mid season (around June) to change to a 1/1 or 2/1 ratio or, if the plants remain dark and tight at the heads and lack vigour, flushing with plain water 2 gallons/sq yd (10 litres/m²) may be necessary. Whether or not thereafter, into July/August, it is necessary to give 2/1 or 3/1 ratio potash/nitrogen will depend on the vigour of the plant. Too much vigour – keep the 3/1 ratio. Too little vigour – drop to 2/1 or even 1/1. A month or so before crop removal, stop feeding entirely and change to plain water only. This programme must be metered according to analysis figures. The ratios of self-made feeds are made up as follows:

Composition of Feeds in oz/gallon and g/litre

Dilution Rate	K_2O to N ratio	Potassium Nitrate	Urea	or	Ammonium Nitrate	PPM N	K_2O
1–200	3–1 high potash	24 oz/gal 150 g/l				105	335
1–200	2–1 standard	24 oz/gal 150 g/l	5 oz/gal 31 g/l	or	6 oz/gal 37 g/l	170	335
1–300	1–1 high nitrogen	24 oz/gal 150 g/l	16 oz/gal 100g/1	or	21 oz/gal 130 g/l	225	225
1–200	1–1½ medium/high nitrogen	24 oz/gal 150 g/l			11 oz/gal 68 g/l	225	335

Note: This is the 'stock' solution prepared by careful mixing in warm water. It is then diluted preferably with a calibrated dilutor. Where straw bale culture is involved it may be found that nitrogen 'lock-up' occurs early in the season, the nitrogen being appropriated by the decomposing straw. Later on there may be an excess of nitrogen. Analysis is advised, altering the feeds accordingly. The most important issue, especially in limited amounts of growing media (as will be the case with grow bags or peat modules), is to avoid the build up of high salt concentrations. This will invariably result in 'black bottoms' (often called blossom end rot, see page 73). Recent years have shown nutrient levels not to be so critical as once thought but really high salt levels are dangerous.

Picking the Fruit

This must be done on a system bearing in mind the markets being served. The fruit should be picked when it is beginning to turn in colour and not left in the hot sun. Grading is necessary according to the standards laid down by the Ministry of Agriculture and Department of Agriculture in the U.K. and the appropriate body in other countries. A chemical called 'Ethrel E' can be used to ripen fruit towards the end of the season and this is used according to directions. At the end of season when it is decided to remove the crop the stems are cut 12 in or so (30 cm) from ground level and disposed of effectively. The roots are then pulled up with as much of the root tissue as possible. Watering may be required with border crops to enable this to take place. All the crop debris should then be taken away from the area of the greenhouse on tractor trailer and either dumped or allowed to dry before burning. It helps if foliage cut off is allowed to wilt for 12–24 hours – as this reduces its bulk. During root removal, examination of the roots should determine whether any pests or diseases have made headway. Houses are washed down and fumigated. Jeyes fluid, Sterizal or formaldehyde are useful here.

Chapter Ten

Crop Economics of Tomatoes

The economics of tomato growing require constant appraisal in relation to price structure at various seasons. A table of prices in Scotland for the years 1976–1979 shows typical patterns, but it must be noted that prices throughout the U.K. are *not* standard and show considerable regional fluctuations. The following are typical figures: (Efford E.H.S. in their trial report (1978) quote yields in excess of 155 t/acre (39 kg/m^2.)

Crop Definition (Southern England)
Early heated
Planted January/early February

Yield
100 ton/acre   46 lb/sq yd
260 tonne/ha   26 kg/m^2

Costs	sq yd	m^2
Plants	3	3.5
Peat	.04 bales	.05 bales
Fuel (oil)	8.5 gallons 38 litres	48 litres
Propane	1.4 kg	1.6 kg
Electricity	.3 units	.4 units
Methyl Bromide	.8 kg	.9 kg
Fertilizers		
Base and liquid feeds	2 lbs	1 kg
Sprays	0.12% of gross income	0.13% of gross income
Water	100 gallons	570 litres
String	.01 kg	.01 kg
Sundries	2.2% of gross income	2.2% of gross income

Marketing Costs = 11% – 12% of gross income

Labour Units
.6 m² per man hour
.7 sq yd per man hour   Growing *and* marketing

For Scotland, figures are broadly similar except for oil which rises sharply to 12 gallons/55 litres per sq yd or 66 litres per sq metre. Economists also point out the lower potential yields due to poorer light intensity.

Later Crops
Planting March

Yields   60 ton/acre *upwards* (150 tonne/ha) = 27 lb/sq yd (15 kg/m², Efford E.H.S. quote 22 kg/m² in their 1978 report)

Fuel   2 gallons (9.12 litres/yd²)
                   (11.4 litres/m²)
                   (+ 30–40% in Scotland)

Labour Units
1.4 sq yd per man hour
1.2 sq m per man hour

Cold Crops
Planting late April

Yield
Very variable according to region, but
 50–60 ton/acre average
125–150 tonne/ha average

Fuel costs
Nil

Labour Units
1.5 sq yd per man hour
1.4 sq m per man hour

In Scotland, the economics of unheated crops are doubtful in a bad cool season, with yields as low as 30–40 ton/acre/75–100 tonne/ha. Note the 'glut' situation which can arise with price patterns (see page 69).

Crop Economics of Tomatoes

Typical Price Check Table

**Tomato Prices – 1976, 1978 and 1979 (Scotland)
pence per lb**

Week ending	1976	1978	1979	Difference 1978/79
March 14	–	–	80	–
21	–	–	70	–
28	–	–	73	–
April 4	–	64	–	–
11	75	78	67	down 11
18	58	55	57	up 2
25	40	50	45	down 5
May 2	30	50	55	up 5
9	28	48	50	up 2
16	32	40	43	up 3
23	30	35	40	up 5
30	29	39	38	down 1
June 6	26	43	39	down 4
13	24	32	39	up 7
20	22	35	40	up 5
27	26	30	30	–
July 4	30	24	23	down 1
11	35	25	33	up 8
18	27	19	31	up 11
25	28	21	25	up 4
Aug 1	28	29	25	down 4
8	27	29	25	down 4
15	20	20	24	up 4
22	11	22	25	up 3
29	11	21	22	up 1
Sept 5	15	23	19	down 4
12	15	24	17	down 7
19	23	19	16	down 3
26	20	19	19	–
Oct 3	9	20	20	–
10	14	17	25	up 8
17	14	20	24	up 4
24	15	16	20	up 4

Chapter Eleven

Pest and Disease Check for Tomatoes

Tomato

Pests
Thrips (mainly *Thrips tabaci*) – other species occasionally troublesome. Wilting and scarring of foliage and fruit is caused by removal of sap – control by spraying foliage with Malathion, or other insecticide.
Aphids (mostly the glasshouse-potato aphid *Aulacorthum solani*, or the peach potato aphid *Myzus perisicae*) – symptoms are yellowing of foliage. Many alternative treatments include spraying with Demeton-S-methyl on young plants, Gamma H.C.H. on mature plants.
Red Spider Mite (*Tetranychus urticae*) – foliage hard, with yellow mottling on upper surface, with 'webbing' on fruit and flowers. Mites breed rapidly in spring, resistance may occur as in aphids and treatment should be varied, for example on seedlings use sprays of Demeton-S-methyl, Dimethoate, etc; on mature plants use Dicofol or smoke with Azobenzene or Tetradifon. To prevent hibernation of mites, remove old crop immediately after fruit finished. Predator may be introduced.
Slaters or woodlice (*Armadilidium spp*) – nocturnal feeders, chewing through at or below soil level the stems of seedlings. Apply Gamma H.C.H. spray to soil.
Root-knot eelworms (*Meloidogyne spp*) – symptoms are pale lower foliage and severe wilting. Large irregular shaped galls on roots. Control by removing damaged plants and roots and sterilize soil or go to alternative cultural system. Note that grafts on 'N' labelled root-stocks are resistant to some species of the pest.
Whitefly (*Trialeurodes vaporariorum*) – these are found in large numbers

on young plants and growing points of old plants. Cause chlorotic areas and honeydew which induces the growth of black moulds. Spray with Malathion or Diazinon, or introduce predators.
Tomato Leafminer (*Liriomyza solani*) – adults feed on foliage causing pits; larvae tunnel into cotyledons of seedlings often killing them. Spray soil and seedlings with Diazinon.
Springtails (*Collembola*) – pin holes or scraping of surface of foliage on seedlings and young plants – apply Gamma H.C.H. dust to soil or drench soil with Gamma H.C.H.
Tomato Moth (*Laconobia oleracea*) – symptoms are skeletonized foliage and holes in fruit and stems and stripping of leaves. Handpicking on young plants instead of spraying, but spray older plants with Dichlovrovs or Trichlorphon at intervals.
Symphilids (*Scutigerella immaculata*) – these pests are fast moving and prefer moist soil. They feed on young roots and encourage infection. Control when found at root system and drench soil with Diazinon or Gamma H.C.H.
Potato-cyst Eelworm (*Globodera rostochiensis*) – dwarf plants will have slight purple discoloration and wilt, with large numbers of fibrous roots near the surface. From mid-summer white or golden pinhead cysts will be visible. Plants may be helped by soiling up and extra water. Efficient soil sterilization carried out the following winter using steam or chemicals, or alternative cultural methods, is essential but eelworm is difficult to control.

Diseases
Grey Mould (*Botrytis cinerea*) – pale brown lesions on stem, with grey fungus. Fruit will have green rings with mark at centre, 'Botrytis spot'. Destroy remains of previous tomato crop. Wash down house with detergent or disinfectant and fumigate. Sterilize canes, boxes and soil before planting. Spray Captan on stem bases and adjacent soil. Avoid checks to plant growth, give good ventilation and a little heat if necessary. Spray with Benomyl or Dichlofluanid after de-leafing on programme basis, preferably as a 'Fog'.
Damping off root and foot rots (*Rhizoctonia solani, Pythium spp, Phytophthora spp*) – symptoms are collapse of seedlings at soil level, roots may be rotted. Control by sterilizing seed boxes, pots and compost and drench with fungicide. Sterilize border soil. Do not plant in cold media.
Stem Rot (*Didymella lycopersici*) – rotting at base of plant and dark lesions at flower end of fruit. Treat as for Grey Mould.
Blight (*Phytophthora infestans*) – brown areas on leaves, with dark streaks on stem. Reddish-brown marbled patches on green fruit which later shrivel and die. Spray regularly with fungicides, reduce humidity by ventilating and giving some heat.

Pest and Disease Check for Tomatoes

Brown Root and Corky Root (*Pyrenochaeta terrestris*) – plants wilt in bright weather and show rot and loss of tissues, with corklike swelling or roots. Sterilize soil, or go to alternative cultural method.

Wilts (*Verticillium albo-astrum, V. Dahliae, Fusarian oxysporum f. sp. lycopersici and F. redolens*) – yellowing and or wilting of leaves, maybe onesided, wood discoloured. Sterilize soil thoroughly. Grow resistant varieties or use plants grafted onto resistant root-stocks.

Bacterial canker (*Corynebacterium michiganense*) – symptoms are brown areas on leaves and yellowish-white mealy areas on stem, spotting on fruit – avoid humidity, remove infected plants and spray with fungicide.

Leaf Mould (*Cladosporium vulvum*) – surface of leaves show patches on upper surface and fur of fungus on lower surface – avoid high humidity and sterilize soil, spraying with Benomyl or Dichlofluanid. Resistant varieties should be grown.

Tomato Mosaic and Streak (*Tobacco mosaic virus*) – seedlings are poor and leaves on older plants distorted, maybe with grey streaks on stem and leaf stalks and markings on fruit. Use virus treated and tested seed, fumigate greenhouse with Formalin or sulphur at end of season. Chemicals are ineffective as a treatment for this virus. Strict hygiene is essential when handling plants. Alternative cultural systems should be considered. Resistant *and* tolerant varieties available.

Magnesium Deficiency – leaves yellow and die gradually from base of plant – spray with magnesium salts, 2% magnesium sulphate.

Iron Deficiency – general yellowish-blanching of leaves with main veins standing out green – adjust pH to less than 7. Apply chelated iron to the soil around affected plants to correct condition.

Aspermy (*Tomato aspermy virus*) – symptoms are distorted foliage, with small fruits. Control aphids which can transmit this virus.

Blossom End Rot (*Black Bottoms*) – dark green circular patch at distal end of fruit, later becoming black. Lack of water can cause this condition, also high salts.

Dry-set – symptom is that fruit fails to set or flowers drop off – treat by damping down during morning on sunny days and use medium application of hormone setting compounds.

'Missing Flowers' – although the truss has formed, this condition is due to excess of nitrogen and low salt content of the soil and unbalanced night/day temperatures. Adjust salt concentration and apply potash to harden growth. Balance day and night temperatures.

Fruit Splitting – this is usually due to irregular water uptake and varying temperatures – even temperatures and regular watering patterns are the answer.

Manganese Toxicity – brownish lesions on stems and petioles, and withering of leaves. Most frequently occurs in acid soils, therefore check pH (if too low adjust to pH 6–6.5 by addition of suitable form of lime).

Pest and Disease Check for Tomatoes

Flower Abortion – possibly related to light input or day/night temperature relationship when flowers are produced which do not have fully viable pollen. Control propagation regime as much as possible, and in poor light areas use supplementary lighting ensuring good conditions.

Greenback – too hard defoliation, lack of potash, or excess sunlight can cause this condition – Moneymaker and other greenback types are recommended, as other types are susceptible. Do not over-defoliate and use shade in hot weather. Increase potash application.

Leaf Curling – as the name implies, leaves curl upwards due to variation in temperature because the plant is unable to use up carbohydrates. Treat by adjusting day/night temperature differential.

Bronzing – symptoms are dead layers of cell below the skin of fruit due to high daytime temperatures, also virus or boron deficiency. This usually affects only a few trusses, but in the meantime avoid high daytime temperatures.

Silvering – this is thought to be a genetical disorder which may correct itself or persist. Up to half the leaves may be affected, showing light-coloured foliage.

Oedema – due to excess humidity, transpiration does not take place rapidly enough through the leaves, giving bumps or blotches. More common on container-grown systems, therefore reduce humidity by avoiding excess water and ensure adequate ventilation.

Buck-Eye Rot (*Phytophora sp*) – grey to reddish-brown patches on fruit. Support lower trusses to prevent fungus splashing from soil on to fruit. Spray soil and lower trusses with copper fungicide.

Flower Drop – this is due to dry atmosphere, lack of moisture or high salt concentration – improve environmental control and check the application of water and nutrients.

Blotchy Ripening – caused by irregular feeding and watering which upsets salt content of the soil, 'vigorous' varieties being the most susceptible. Regular feeding, watering and even temperature should be ensured.

Other Virus Diseases (*spotted wilt virus, cucumber mosaic virus, etc.*) – control aphids and thrips which transmit some of the viruses.

Chapter Twelve

Cucumbers

See also **Gherkins** (page 119)

This is a popular salad crop in many parts of the world. It is a tender annual grown for its fruit which will thrive only under warm conditions and will not withstand any frost. The use of the cucumber fruit is mainly in salads but it is also in demand for mixed pickles.

History
This is another vegetable the origin of which is surrounded in some mystery, as it has been cultivated for some thousands of years. Probably it is a native of Asia and Africa. There is much written about the cucumber in ancient Greek and Roman literature, whereas in Europe it was known in France in the 9th century, and common in England in the 14th century. Commercial cultivation under glass started in England in 1886. It belongs to the genus *cucumis* of which there are 20–25 species, but only two – *Cucumis sativus* and *C. melo* (melon) are of much economic importance. *C. anguia*, called West Indian Gherkin (see page 119), also enjoys some popularity. Cucumbers are normally monoecious, bearing separate male and female flowers but cross-pollination is undesirable as it results in sour malformed fruits, necessitating the removal of male flowers. This chore has been eliminated by the breeding of all 'female' varieties.

Statistics

Cropped Areas (source MAFF) in U.K.
A figure of 588 acres (238 hectares) is given in the June 1980 census with a forecast figure of 595 acres (241 hectares) for 1980. This upward trend is expected to continue.

Figures show a gradual rise both for production in the U.K. and of imports mainly from the Netherlands between March and October, and

76 Cucumbers

from Spain and the Canaries between November and February. Imports are shifting in favour of Mediterranean countries and with high fuel prices in the early 1980s, this is a trend which seems likely to continue – to the possible detriment of U.K. production.

Seed Facts
Seed size is variable according to variety but there are approximately 30 per gram. Germination percentage is usually fairly high, 75–85% or above under ideal conditions. For bed planting at 18 in (45 cm) spaces, approximately 4,000 plants per acre (9884/ha) are required so seed requirements would be 180 g. For denser cordon planting at 15 in (425 cm) plant density could be around 6,000–7,000 plants per acre (17,500/ha). In broad figures plan for 40 g per 1,000 plants as this allows for selection of best seedlings.

Programme of Production
Due attention must be paid to economics of the crop, which are given later. There must be an assessment of economic viability based on previous records, current inflationary trends, changes in marketing strategy locally in the U.K., noting the vulnerability of warm fuel-demanding crops to imports from warm countries overseas. The following is an approximate timetable for northern Europe. It is advisable to batch-sow seed every 2–3 days to given continuity of potting.

Early Crops
For good light areas only and in *well-heated* glass.

Propagation Period:	Approx. 8 weeks
Sow seed:	From late October until December
Potting on:	7–10 days after germination or sooner if need be
Planting:	From mid-December until end-February
Cropping:	February/March until September

Mid-season Crops

Propagation period:	6–7 weeks
Sow seed:	Throughout January
Potting on:	7–8 days after germination or sooner if necessary
Planting:	Throughout March
Cropping:	April onwards

Cucumbers

Late Crops

Propagation period:	4–5 weeks
Sow seed:	February/March
Potting on:	2–8 days after germination
Planting:	April on into May for frames or cloches
Cropping:	April–October

Use of artificial light from October to early March will generally reduce propagating period by 1–2 weeks or more (12 hour batching).

Hygiene
Strict hygiene is essential – clean soil, clean pots or boxes, clean premises, etc., as cucumbers, especially when young, are highly susceptible to weak parasitic diseases. Ensure also that the glass is clean to let in maximum light.

Compost
A variety of composts can be used, but best results come from an open, porous type, adding some coarse grit if need be to improve drainage. Nutrition is *not* important for germination (see Chapter 17).

Sowing Procedure
Put seeds individually on their sides into small pots or paper tubes (contained in trays), small peat pots or seed trays, 40–48 seeds per tray. Soil/peat blocks may also be used (various sizes). Seed should have ½ in (1.2 cm) covering of compost. Now cover with black polythene or paper to induce humidity.

Alternatively place seed in trays on wet blotting paper and cover. Germinate the seed at 80°F (27°C) – usually in a propagating case, or germinating cabinet if this is available. As soon as germination takes place (2–5 days) give plenty of light. Pot up the blotting paper germinated seeds with tweezers immediately they have 'burst'. Note that the seed is best sown in batches. Chitted seed can be bought from seed merchants and in modern terms is frequently put directly in soil/peat blocks.

Seeds of root-stock (*cucurbita ficifolia*) are available which are resistant to wilt diseases; sow these 5–7 days *before* the variety in the same way. Grafting procedure is similar to that practised for tomatoes (see page 36) and is best done when stems are thick enough to handle, making cuts downward and upward in the root-stock and variety stems respectively and binding them with transparent sticky tape. They are then re-potted.

78 **Cucumbers**

Potting

Young seedlings in tubes or peat pots are grown on for a period before potting into 4½ – 5 in (around 12 cm) pots of peat or plastic. Alternatively, with later sowings, seed can be put directly into larger pots or blocks to avoid transplanting. Grow the plants at 70°F (21°C) days and 66°F (18°C) nights after germination has occurred. Box-grown seedlings are moved into pots as soon as practical, and while intermediate 'potting' in pots or soil/peat blocks has been advised in the past, labour costs are such that 'final' potting is now practised as with the later sowings.

Compost for final potting should be John Innes No. 1½ in winter, John Innes No. 2 in spring, or peat/sand equivalent (see Chapter 17). Pot only loosely, avoiding *firm* potting, handling plants with extreme care to avoid stem damage. Keep pots 'tight' initially then space out to around 12 × 12 inches (30 × 30 cm) on an open bench preferably. Feed with *weak* liquid feed at 1:400 medium potash (see Chapter 16). Support plants with small canes when large enough. (See also Rock Wool, Chapter 15.)

Artificial Illumination

Opinions differ on the value of artificial light for cucumbers. Fluorescent tube rigs are generally used similar to tomatoes on a double batch system on greenhouse benches, giving 12–24 hours light daily at around 15,000 lx for 10 days after pricking off (change over at 10 and 22 hours (15 days for chitted seed in soil/peat blocks). Temperatures lit 24 hours 68–78°F (20–25°C). Batch treatment lit 75°F (24°C), unlit 70°F (21°C).

CO_2 Enrichment

There is no great evidence that CO_2 enrichment is of much value for cucumbers at the potting stage or in cropping. This is because the natural complement of CO_2 is added to by the decomposing organic matter in most cultural systems at the cropping stage.

Preparation of Growing Quarters

As with propagation, strict attention to hygiene is imperative in the growing quarters, necessitating washing down of houses, fumigation and other associated issues. Carry over of fungal diseases from previous crops is a constant hazard with the highly susceptible cucumber. There are various cultural systems employed:

(1) *Raised beds* – in a perfect drainage situation, putting gravel or sand below the beds if necessary to achieve this. Beds are made up with layers of well-rotted farmyard manure, 20–24 in wide (50–60 cm) and 6 in (15 cm) deep, on top of which is put a 4 in (10 cm) layer of sterilized soil (see page 164) and previous crop litter followed by further

layers of manure and soil until the beds are up to 20 in (50 cm) high with flat tops. These beds are made up two weeks before planting time and well watered a week or so before planting to induce rapid fermentation. Beds are usually run along the outside wall of smaller greenhouses or 5 ft (1.5 m) apart in Venlo or larger greenhouses on a 'block' basis. Peat is now widely used in place of manure.

(2) *Straw bales* – this involves placement of straw bales in conveniently spaced rows on polythene to isolate the straw from any infection from the soil. It is a highly effective, under-rated system. Heat is put on in the greenhouse to achieve 50–55°F (10–13°C) and the bales thoroughly soaked before applying approximately ¾ lb (350 g) per cwt/50 kg straw of ammonium nitrate lime (26%) and flushed in. This can if necessary be followed by another ¾ lb (350 g) in 3 days and a further 1½ lbs (680 g) of a complete fertilizer containing trace elements. This is a total of 3 lb fertilizer (1.3 kg). ADAS recommend ¾ lb (350 g) Ammonium Nitrate Lime (26%), ¾ lb (350 g) Triple Superphosphates, ¾ lb (350 g) Potassium Nitrate, 8 oz (225 g) Magnesium Sulphate. (A total of 2¾ lb/1.27 kg.) Alternatively, soak the bales with a complete liquid feed such as Maxicrop over a period as this has been found highly satisfactory. The bales should 'heat' and are ready for planting when the temperature has dropped to around 80–90°F (27–32°C). Straw wads can be used with appropriate amounts of fertilizer, contained in polythene troughs.

Fertilizer recommendations to achieve 'heating' vary enormously and in the writer's experience are not critical; more nitrogen may need to be added to induce 'heating'.

(3) *Grow bags and rock wool* – both grow bags and rock wool systems (see Chapter 15) may be used for cucumber culture. Grow bags are laid out on black/white polythene in a similar manner to tomatoes.

(4) *Hydroponics* – cucumbers can be grown on N.F.T. systems although vascular diseases have proved to be a problem in some instances.

(5) *Isolated beds, boxes or large pots* – this tends to involve shorter term culture on benches or in cleared propagation houses.

Nutritional Standards

Border Culture
The following is the ADAS Scale:

Nitrogen (N)	Index 1–2	*(26–100 ppm/mg/litre)
Phosphate (P)	Index 4–5	*(71–100 ppm/mg/litre)
Potash (K)	Index 4	*(405–600 ppm/mg/litre)
Magnesium (Mg)	Index 4	*(176–250 ppm/mg/litre)

*Varies according to extraction method.

80 **Cucumbers**

Nutritional needs for manure/soil beds: *Nitrogen* – total requirement in season 1,000 lbs (454 kg) per acre allowing for drainage. Of those 500 lbs (272 kg) is obtainable from manure, the deficit being made up with 1 oz (28–30 g) per yd/m run of bed of nitro chalk or similar applied every 12–14 days from approximately six weeks after planting. A similar amount of nitrogen can be obtained by giving liquid feed with 200 ppm nitrogen applied at every watering or 100 ppm at alternate waterings. This mixture can be obtained by dissolving 17 oz ammonium nitrate in 1 gallon (100 g/litre) as a stock solution diluting this at 1/200. For straw bales modification to this recommendation would normally be required applying 4–1 nitrogen/potash feed 100 ppm (mg/litre), N 25 ppm (mg/litre), K every watering or 200 ppm (mg/litre), N 50 ppm (mg/litre), K at alternate waterings (see page 163).

Phosphates
The requirement during the season for the crop is approximately 200 lbs (90 kg) per acre. Soil usually contains sufficient reserve for this quantity to be met especially when mixed with farmyard manure. For straw bales the requirement is met by using the phosphates detailed as for straw bale treatment.

Potash
The requirements are in the region of 600–700 lbs (272–317 kg) per acre. There is usually sufficient reserve in the soil or manure but only a proportion of this is available. Generally speaking the addition of potash is not required during the early season where straw bale culture is practised, but because, although sufficient potash may be added at the outset, much of this is lost by drainage or 'lock up' and a normal requirement from 8 weeks after planting would be 1 oz sulphate of potash (28/30 g) per yd/m run of bed at 4 weekly intervals, or liquid feed as detailed under nitrogen. Necessary feed for this may be obtained by dissolving 17 oz ammonium nitrate and 3 oz potassium nitrate in 1 gallon of water (100 g/litre ammonium nitrate and 18g/litre potassium nitrate) diluting this at 1/100 or 1/200 as required, according to whether crops are fed every watering or alternate watering.

Lime (Calcium)
The pH of the soil should be brought up to around 6.5 and if necessary ground limestone should be used to achieve this figure. On straw bale culture pH is usually sufficiently high by the addition of the ammonium nitrate/lime when this is used.

Magnesium
Whether to apply magnesium or not is a matter for soil analysis. Mag-

Cucumbers

nesium can be added to straw bales but the plant supply can be met also by using a trace element containing fertilizer or complete liquid feeds.

Planting

Set out the cucumbers when 12–15 in (30–37 cm) high at a suitable distance apart, generally 15–21 in (40–53cm) according to the system adopted. Do not plant with an 'air pocket' below the root ball, and note that with bales and rock wool the plants are left on the surface. Where soil/manure beds are involved, leave the plant a little proud of the surface to improve drainage and avoid stem diseases. With straw bales run a ridge of compost or peat along the top of the bales and merely cover the root ball. Water the plants in well and keep the atmosphere reasonably humid especially during the establishment period, although modern tendencies are to avoid the very high humidities previously recommended in view of disease risk. Temperatures should be around 70°F (21°C) day and 66°F (19°C) night, ventilating at around 80°F (27°C).

Training

A variety of training systems can be evolved according to the method of planting, and types of greenhouse and facilities.

Arch Training

When the plants are grown up the sides to the 'centre' of the greenhouse or arch which is provided. This is the 'traditional' method of growing and training. When the plants are set out the cane securing the plant is tied on to the bottom wire, but the plant stem is taken inside the wire so that there will be a bit of 'give' to avoid pulling the plant out of the bed. The leading shoot is allowed to reach the top wire when it is then stopped, being tied in as it progresses. Train side shoots which will arise every 5–6 in (12–15 cm) 4–5 weeks after planting and stop these beyond the second leaf. Sub-laterals will arise from these and these are stopped two leaves and tied in. Plant training and pruning is a constant job and will constitute the major labour requirement especially where arch training is involved. Cordon training is much less labour intensive (45–50% less) (see Figure 6a).

Cordon Training

This takes two forms: oblique or V-shaped cordons (where the plants are grown at an angle (see Figures 6b and 6c) but kept to a single main stem which is twisted round string which is looped around a plant hook, pushed into the bed. It is important to leave a loop or a bend in the stem to avoid damage to roots. Laterals as they develop are shortened

82 Cucumbers

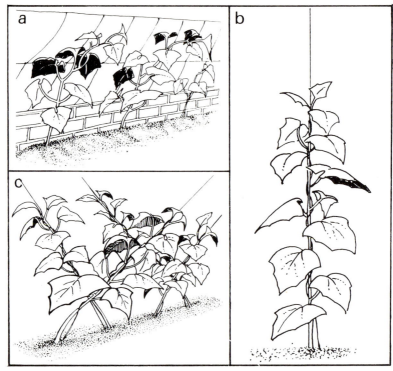

Figure 6 Training system for cucumbers
6a Training on arch systems
6b Vertical string method
6c 'V' systems

and nowadays with 'all female' varieties there is no great effort made to train the plants in a highly specific fashion. All that is required is to keep them in reasonable order by cutting out surplus shoots and shortening trailing stems, it being important to avoid making contact with beds. If using 'normal' varieties (not 'all female') the plants' male flowers must be removed regularly to avoid pollination.

Calculation of Water Needs

The amount of water needed by the cucumber crops depends largely on the amount of light they receive which in practical terms means how sunny it is. Irrigation requirements are regularly estimated from readings at experimental horticultural stations in England and Wales and this technique is fairly widespread throughout Europe. While they are estimates, they are very useful in assessing the quantity of water required. Adjustments must be made for the height of crop and type of glasshouse. The figures tend to vary from year to year and the following can *merely be taken as a 'high' average.*

January	13,000 gallons/acre	146,042 litres/ha
February	17,000 gallons/acre	190,978 litres/ha
March	47,000 gallons/acre	527,998 litres/ha
April	50,000 gallons/acre	561,700 litres/ha
May	74,000 gallons/acre	831,316 litres/ha
June	80,000 gallons/acre	898,720 litres/ha
July	80,000 gallons/acre	898,720 litres/ha
August	80,000 gallons/acre	898,720 litres/ha
September	60,000 gallons/acre	674,040 litres/ha
October	30,000 gallons/acre	337,020 litres/ha
November	15,000 gallons/acre	168,510 litres/ha
December	8,000 gallons/acre	89,872 litres/ha
TOTAL	554,000 gallons/acre	6,223,636 litres/ha

Note that these figures relate to the Southern part of the U.K. Obviously water in this quantity must be available in the first case and the system of applying the water must be efficient. Much will depend on the method of cultivation. For beds and straw bales there is a lot to be said for spray lines, while for isolated bed and rock wool systems, trickle lines are much more effective, if indeed, not essential. Evaporimeters linked to solonoid valves is an ideal way of controlling water application. For supply of liquid feeding an efficient dilutor must be available.

Mulching

Traditional crops on beds tend to become compacted and for this reason mulching is carried out on two or three occasions throughout the season. Mulches of stable manure or long straw manure should be spread in a shallow layer over the surface of the bed when the white roots are seen. It is important to avoid close contact with the stem of the plant, otherwise rotting may occur. Straw can be used instead of manure and this has the advantage of not decomposing so quickly.

Necking Up

This involves placing a small mound of soil or peat a few inches (10 cm) in depth around the base of the stem to encourage new roots. Neither mulching nor necking up have of course any application for rock wool systems (see page 145) or apply when plants are grown in grow bags.

Cucumbers

Harvesting
Cucumbers are ready when the diameter of the fruit is even through its full length and the tip stops extending. The fruit should be cut at the supporting stalk with a sharp knife, leaving a short piece of stalk. The fruit must be kept cool after picking. It is then graded according to the standards of the country concerned, and marketed in cardboard trays lined with paper.

Frame and Cloche Culture
Cucumbers make an ideal and lucrative crop to follow lettuce in frames or cloches. Raise the plants as previously described but note that planting in frames or cloches will not normally take place until April or May. Plants can be produced very quickly (2–3 weeks) by sowing direct in peat pots. Seed can be sown directly in the frame. The number of cucumbers to plant per frame depends on size, but generally two plants per Dutch light sash or per two or three cloches is adequate. Plant either at the corners or in the centre of frames after taking out a planting hole 12 in wide × 9 in deep (30 × 22.5 cm) and fill in with a mixture of well-rotted manure and good soil. Paint the glass with whitewash above the plant position to avoid sun scorch and help establishment. Keep the plants merely to reasonable proportions and spread a layer of straw on the base of the frame or cloche so that the cucumbers are not spoiled. Remove male flowers (if not female varieties) when they form to avoid pollination and water and feed regularly.

Crop Economics

Crop Definition
Modified arch
Planting February
Straw bales
Plant spacing
21 in (53 cm)

Actual Yield
44–56 lb/sq yd/25–32 kg/m^2

Cucumbers

According to Region

	sq yd	m²
Plants (Varies a lot according to spacing)	.7–.8	.8–.9
Peat	.02 bales	.03 bales
Fuel (oil)	9 gals	51 litres
Electricity (variable)	.08 units	.1 units
Straw bales	15 lbs	8 kg
Water (very variable)	80 gals	450 litres
Fertilizer (average)	1½ lbs	600 g
Sprays	1% of gross revenue	1% of gross revenue
String	¾ oz	22 g
Sundries	½% of gross revenue	

Marketing Costs = 13–14% of gross revenue

Labour Units
1 man hour per sq. yd
1 man hour per .8 m²

Crop Definition
Crop cold (Not always viable in northern U.K.)
Plant early June
Soil/manure beds
Cordon grown

Actual Yield
24 lb/sq yd/14 kg/m²

	sq yd	m²
Plants	1.4	1.8
Manure (FYM)	17 lbs	10 kg
Fertilizers (average)	7–10 oz	200–300 kg
Sprays	.75% of revenue	.8% of revenue
Water (very variable)	60 gals	340 litres
Sterilizers (very variable)	1% of gross revenue	1% of gross revenue
Sundries	1½–2% of gross revenue	½ of gross revenue

Marketing costs = 13–14% of gross revenue

Labour Units
1 man hour per 2.4 sq yd
1 man hour per 2 m²

86 Cucumbers

Pest Disease and Disorder Check

Trouble	Description and Symptoms	Control
Aphids especially *Aphis gossypii*, melon or cotton aphid	Puckering, distortion and yellowing of leaves. Honey dew exudations.	Systemic insecticides on young plants. *Spray* Demeton – S – methyl, dimetheoate formothion, Oxydemeton methyl, Parathion (not fully systemic) and others. For cropping plants spray with Dimetheoate, Formothion, Malathion, Derris or Nicotine. For *Atomising* Diazinon or Malathion. *Smokes* Nicotine or Parathion. Note that it is advisable to vary control to avoid resistance build up.
White Fly *trialeurodes vaporariorum*	Mothlike insects on leaves – wilting of leaves and honey dew exudations very weakening.	Spray or smoke young plants with Parathion. For mature plants repeated sprays of Malathion or Diazinon. Due to resistance build up consider biological control (*Ercarsia Formosa*).
Millepeds oxidus gracilis	Stem and root damage. Disease entry is allowed.	Use soil drenches of Gamma HCH or Malathion.
Red Spider Mite *Tetranychus urticae*	Females hibernate in cracks and crevices in greenhouse – emerge when temperature rises and then feed on leaves causing speckling, wilting, and death in severe cases. High levels of infection are necessary to reduce crops greatly.	Spray *young plants* with range of systemic materials including Demeton – S – methyl, dimetheoate, Formothion or Oxydemeton methyl or non-systemic Parathion. Older plants use sprays of Diazinon dicofol, Tetrafodin, petroleum oil (care,) Quinmethiote. Biological control is highly effective.
Fungus gnats *Bradysia* species	Damage to roots slows up growth and may cause death. Mites also feed on foliage. Larvae transparent or white in colour with a blackish head.	Make sure plants are not short of water and drench beds with Malathion. Should not be a problem if soil is sterilized or other cultural systems used.
French Fly *Tyrophagus neiswanderi*	Mites will feed on young plants causing tiny holes on leaves. Severe attack can cause shoots to go blind. Mites may be visible as creamy white globe-shaped organisms with many bristles.	As the mites are brought in with straw and manure this is a pest unlikely with other cultural systems. When attack does occur spray with Diazinon or Dicofol.

Cucumbers

Trouble	Description and Symptoms	Control
Root-knot eelworm *Meloidogyne hapla* and other species	Plants will wilt in sunlight and lower foliage will turn yellow. Very large swollen roots will develop almost like club root. Very much a problem of warm conditions especially in arid countries. In places like Egypt the eelworm comes in with the Nile irrigation water.	Absolute cleanliness is necessary and should attack occur very careful sterilization with heat or DD injection will be required although there can be problems with DD on a heavy type of soil. If severe attack is suspected then go on to alternative cultural methods as there are no resistant rootstocks.
Symphilids *Scutigerella immaculata*	Small white organisms about 6mm long, 12 pairs of legs. Feed on young roots and cause the plant to wilt and go blue. They are very active in a moist soil.	Drench soil with Gamma HCH or Diazinon.
Thrips Various spp but mainly *Thrips tabaci*	The insects suck sap and cause scarring of the foliage. They also mark the fruit. More important perhaps they spread virus. They are yellow-brown insects with narrow wings.	Regular spraying with Malathion, timing any two applications within a 14-day period.
Woodlice *Armadillidium spp*	These can cause serious bother, plants being eaten off at soil level or the growth of the plant severely stunted by root damage. Woodlice have typical segmented bodies with numbers of small legs.	Spray with Gamma HCH making sure all rubbish has been removed.
Black root rot *Phomopsis sclerotioides*	Rotting takes place on stem base and roots and plant wilts and dies. Black spots appear on tissues of smaller roots and larger older roots become blackened.	Sterilization of soil is necessary or grow on straw bales.
Stem and root rots *Rhizoctonia spp,* *Pythium spp,* *Phytophthora spp*	Young plants show light or dark brown lesions at stem bases. Rotting takes place of roots.	Sterilization of soil is necessary. Application of Quintozene dust to surface of beds may be carried out and raked in. Diseased plants may have to be removed and Copper Fungicide applied to base of remaining plants.

88 Cucumbers

Trouble	Description and Symptoms	Control
Black stem rot *Mycosphaerella melonis*	Green spots appear on leaves which turn brown. The edges of the leaves become water-soaked and soft greyish green rot at end of fruit.	Glasshouse should be thoroughly cleaned out and all debris destroyed. Reduction in humidity helps and all diseased growth should be cut out. At first sign of disease spray with Thiram or Zineb and then at 14-day intervals. Thiram may be dusted on.
Mosaic *Cucumber mosaic virus*	Distortion of leaves and fruit showing yellow and green mosaic.	Spray with insecticide to control aphid sectors after destroying young infected plants.
Gummosis *Cladosporium cucumerimum*	Sticky liquid appears on sunken spots of young fruit. Fruit becomes split showing inner tissues.	Reduction of humidity helps and low temperatures should be avoided. Affected fruit should be destroyed. Spray with Thiram, Captan or Zineb at 10-day intervals.
Green mottle *Cucumber green mottle virus*	Not too noticeable mottling on young shoot leaves and no symptoms on older leaves or fruits. Crop yield can show a marked loss.	Easily transmitted by handling as disease is seed-borne. Affected plants should be destroyed, also adjacent plants. Hands and utensils should be washed with Trisodium phosphate (5%).
Powdery mildew *Erysiphe cichoracearum*	A white powdery growth appears on leaves.	Drench soil with Dimethirimol. Sprays such as Colloidal copper sulphur, benomyl, Dinocap or Quinomethionate may be applied at 14-day intervals.
Grey mould *Botrytis cinerea*	Lesions at nodes are water-soaked and scarring on leaves. Fruit becomes rotted.	Reduction of humidity helps. Infected tissue should be removed and spraying with Benomyl may be carried out.
Truffle Fungus	Development of fungus in straw bales.	Difficult to deal with without crop damage. Change source of bales for future.

Tomato crops are only economically viable if yields and quality of fruit are consistently high, as here. *(D. T. Brown & Co Ltd, Blackpool)*

A modern mobile lighting installation for cucumbers and tomatoes at Clydegrove Nursery, Crossford, Lanarkshire, Scotland. *(South of Scotland Electricity Board)*

The straw bale culture system of tomatoes tends to have been ousted by Grow Bags or N.F.T. but it may still have application in some instances if clean straw bales uncontaminated by weed-killers are available at reasonable cost. Bales can be used for cucumbers and other crops with good effect. *(Horticulture Industry Weekly)*

Raising tomato plants for sale is big business but growing conditions must be good in modern automatically ventilated glasshouses. *(Horticulture Industry Weekly)*

Grow Bags are widely used for tomato culture in Britain. A training 'cage' is used to good effect in this instance but there are many modifications.
(Horticulture Industry Weekly)

Double skinned black plastic structures are ideal for housing lighting rigs because of their heat conservation properties. This installation was at Richlands Nursery, Cleghorn, Lanarkshire, Scotland. It is an ideal arrangement for bedding plant producers wanting to keep capital spending low.
(South of Scotland Electricity Board)

More and more crops are being grown in warm climates under protection, such as in Saudi Arabia where air conditioned fibreglass structures and nutrient film technique systems are widely used. *(Both pictures by courtesy of Canadian Hydro Gardens Ltd)*

Mobile glasshouses were at one time the latest method of cropping to avoid 'soil sickness' problems. Here is an early Dutch mobile glasshouse where only the roof moved over permanent gutters. This picture was taken when the author made a European study of mobile glasshouses in the 60's.

Lettuce crops must be of high quality if they are to be accepted by the public. *(D. Van der Ploeg, Elite Zaden B. V., Barendrecht, Holland)*

Intensive lettuce production in 27 foot wide plastic structure. *(Clovis Lande Assoc Ltd, Hildenborough, Kent)*

A plastic structure with twin spray lines makes an ideal lettuce production unit at low capital cost. This is an 18 × 123 feet Solar Dome. *(Clovis Lande Assoc Ltd, Hildenborough, Kent)*

Peppers grown in borders can be a lucrative 'catch' crop. *(Photograph by the author)*

Vegetable plants can be raised and sold in Jiffy 7's. For smaller growers not wishing to become involved with using soil blocks, the Jiffys are an ideal marketing module. This picture was taken at Kirton E.H.S. in the late 60's. *(Jiffy Pots (UK) Ltd)*

Celery production in plastic multi-bay units. *(Clovis Lande Assoc Ltd, Hildenborough, Kent)*

Sheet steaming has many applications for borders or raised beds. This picture was taken at Efford E.H.S. England. *(Ministry of Agriculture, Fisheries and Food)*

Chapter Thirteen

Lettuce Under Glass or Plastic

Many years ago lettuce production in temperate zones tended to be confined largely to summer production out of doors. There was first of all development into growing of spring lettuce and autumn lettuce under protection. Now in recent years there has been a swing to produce high quality lettuce under protection on a 'programmed' basis for the full year. This has been made possible in two ways. By 'short day' varieties, specially bred to grow in poor light conditions during the short winter days. Simultaneously varieties have been developed which are able to stand heat or 'stress' during the summer without quickly 'bolting' or running to seed in 'long day' conditions (see page 91).

The key factors for production are good light transmitting, drip-free structures (glass or plastic), weed-free soil (strict disease control or provision for N.F.T.) (see Chapter 15), irrigation with spray lines and, for year-round production, mild heat for winter and adequate ventilation for summer. Excess temperatures or humidity are not desirable so where plastic structures or frames are used, good ventilation is important to avoid this. Pest and disease control is also essential, especially the latter, and breeders have been busy by providing varieties which are resistant to various races of downy mildew (Bremia), and in addition new chemicals and application methods are promising.

Historical and Botanical
As far as is known, lettuce is a native of Europe and Asia and has been cultivated for over 2,500 years. The cultivated lettuce is *Lactuca sativa* and this is closely related to the wild lettuce *Lactuca scariola* which is a common weed in various countries. These two readily cross-fertilize which leads some botanists to believe they belong to the same species, hence the name *Lactuca scariola var sativa*.

They are basically 'long day' plants in their original form which will not flower unless the day length exceeds 12 hours. Genetically they are diploids. Lettuce is an annual and a composite. There are four main species.

Lactuca Sativa Var Capitata	Head or Cabbage Lettuce
L Sativa Var Crispa	Cutting or Leaf Lettuce
L Sativa Var Longifolia	Cos Lettuce
L Sativa Var Augustana	Asparagus Lettuce

In the U.K. there are records of cabbage lettuce being produced in the 16th century, and then of course there was the famous 'Terreaux' area around Paris where lettuce growing featured prominently, intercropped with carrots and other crops. Lettuce growing on a large scale under protection and over a long period appears to have had a very varied reception by producers for many years owing to the inability of most varieties then available to 'heart' properly under the 'artificial' conditions of poor light imposed on them in winter, or conversely in the summer the high temperature problems. It was the 'Dutch light' influence in the East of England in the 1930s which undoubtedly set the scene for intensive growing systems, and today lettuce growing under protection is a very considerable industry.

Statistics of Crop

A fairly static situation would appear to exist in protected crop areas. Figures provided by the Ministry of Agriculture and Fisheries and Food for the United Kingdom give a figure of about 3,513 acres (1,422 hectares) for 1980 and a similar figure for 1981. This figure has not appreciably altered in 6 years and is likely to hold true for the near future.

Lettuce is being grown in low heat input newly erected glass in North Humberside and under unheated plastic structures generally. Figures for lettuce and endive imported into the U.K. by the Ministry unfortunately do not differentiate between protected and outdoor crops but quantities show a rise of 90% between 1977 and 1978 from 10,600 tonnes to 12,000 tonnes respectively and it seems likely that this trend will continue.

Light Levels or Solar Radiation in Relation to Production Regions

Within the U.K. the selection of 'good light' areas is of significance for many crops especially those such as lettuce where production continues throughout the winter months.

Absence of industrial pollution, reflection from large water bulks along with freedom from low cloud periods are factors which have not entirely been followed when one looks at the 'pockets' of production

Lettuce Under Glass or Plastic 91

which have developed in North Humberside (East Riding), and Lancashire or Sussex would seem to be a much more logical place to set up winter lettuce production. Nor can it be said that the Westland area of Holland where considerable areas of glass produce winter lettuce is climatically ideal. This region, while enjoying good natural light, still suffers a lot from coastal fogs and mists especially in the winter months. Obviously flat land for easy mechanization and proximity to markets is also important, with such a highly perishable crop.

Enterprise Selection

Lettuce can form a part of the cropping cycle, or it can be considered as a full year enterprise. There can be so many ways of crop management that levels of capital investment and profitability vary enormously. The scene is also a changing one and new cultural systems arise all the time. Coupled with this (and of course this related to all protected cropping) rising fuel and labour prices confuse matters still further. In the early 1980s low fuel input is the theme for lettuce.

In the costings given at the end of this section it is important to look at the key issues which centre around fuel and labour.

Lettuce Varieties

It is a critical matter to select the correct variety for the season of production. Intensive breeding programmes result in a flood of new varieties, each with their own inbuilt character and requirements in terms of seasonability, heat and to a lesser extent nutrient levels. Testing of varieties goes on at various centres throughout the world and in the U.K. principally at the National Institute of Agricultural Botany (N.I.A.B.) and research stations.

Lists of seed firms are given in the Appendix.

Production

Seed Facts
Important Note:
Much of the information given relates to production out of doors but, as the situation regarding cultural methods is a rapidly changing one, as full a picture as possible of seed sizes and quantities has been given. The situation regarding seeds is also changing.

Pelleted Seeds

There are three types of 'pelleted' seed and availability varies according to variety.

'Filcoat'

Mainly used for direct sowing out of doors with suitably sized Stanhay

Lettuce Under Glass or Plastic

Ribbed belt hole size *15 base C choke A Webb Cell Wheel EP for regular size.
  6,000 – 8,000 pellets per lb (pellets per oz 375–500)
  13,000 – 17,000 per kg (pellets per 10 g 110–170 for new size around 100 per 10 g)
*Rate per acre at normal sowing spacings:
  4 in (10 cm) by 12 in (30 cm) rows
  18–20 lbs (8–10 kg)
  22–24 kg/ha

'Minicoat' Pellets
*Size 1½–3 mm oval. Stanhay Belt/Hole size 12/base Z-choke T Webb Cell Wheel G
*20,000 – 30,000 per lb (44,000 – 60,000 per kg)
Pellets per 100 g 440–600 (Pellets per oz 1,250–1,875)
More difficult to sow with precision because of oval shape
*Rate per acre at 4 × 12 in (10 × 30 cm) 6–7 lbs (7–7.5 kg/ha)

'Split Pills'*
Size 3 × 3.5 mm oval seed splits in half to allow emergence of seedling Invariably used for soil/peat blocks under protection (also used outdoors)
*Pellets per 10 g 200–300. Pellets per oz 600–800. Invariably sold by number (not weight)
Plant at 8 × 8 in (20 × 20 cm)
*98,000 per acre = 246,000 per ha reduced to 58,000–65,000 actual plants per acre of glass (143,300–160,600 ha)
*Stanhay Ribbed Belt/Hole Size 14.5/base C/choke A Webb Cell Wheel EP

Natural Seed
Approx 7,000–12,000 per 10 g

Germination Temperatures and Percentages
Germination Temperatures 50°–60°F (10°–15°C)
Dormancy Breaking Temperatures 48 hours at 40°F (4.4°C)
Optimum Germination Temperatures 62°F (16°C)
Germination percentage 75%

Lettuce pellets vary in size and it is always advisable to check up with suppliers when purchasing equipment for sowing them.

Lettuce Under Glass or Plastic

Programme for Production

Time from sowing to cropping under good cultural conditions depends basically on temperature and light levels – as poor light conditions can delay cropping – discourage hearting – and result in loss of weight. It ranges from 150 days in winter (in poor light areas) down to 50–55 days* in 'summer' (including late spring – early autumn).

In practical terms this means that production schedules cannot be entirely reliable and are very weather- and region-dependent.

'Growing room' propagation can, however, do much to maintain schedules at the propagating stage as seedlings can be produced on a set timetable irrespective of light levels and allow a batch to be ready to follow a crop which is seen to be almost ready for market. Batches under lights in blocks can be left for 'extra' time, if space allows.

Approximate Timetables

Important Note:
Depending on plant development, according to variety, region, weather and light. Growing room raising will shorten propagation periods.

*Sowing	Planting	Harvesting
Autumn Crop		
1st August	14th Sept.	20th Sept.
to	to	to
25th August	8th Oct.	31st Dec.
Winter Crop		
20th Sept.	13th Oct.	1st Jan.
to	to	to
1st Oct.	28th Oct.	15th Feb.
Early Spring Crop (Especially light sensitive)		
10th Oct.	16th Nov.	Mid Feb.
to	to	to
20th Oct.	10th Dec.	Early April
Spring Crop		
1st Nov.	Mid Dec.	Mid March
to	to	to
late Feb.	late March	Mid May
Summer Crop		
From 1st March at intervals	10–14 days later	Approx. 50–60 days after sowing

*Note the time savings now possible with pre-germinated seed.

94 Lettuce Under Glass or Plastic

Crop Definition	Timing (See p. 93)	Heating, Ventilation, Watering, etc.	Notes
'Autumn' heated or cold. *Note* Seed best sown in batches of 2–4 day intervals.	As per table (page 93). Sowing from 1st August to 25th August. Harvesting can be considerably delayed in poor light areas and cold weather (if no heat).	Heating costs low in mild seasons. Little ventilation until plants established in moist regime. Only water early in day. 'Average' min. temp. around 40–45°F (4–7°C) night. 'Boosting' with CO_2 and high temperature is usual practice. Ventilate at 65–68°F (18–20°C) according to CO_2 input.	Warm autumns can 'spoil' crop and hinder hearting. High risk of frost damage with unheated crop; also diseases in high humidity situation. Usually a fair demand for good quality.
'Winter' heated or 'forced' in good light. *Note* Seed sown in batches of 4 days.	As per table. Sowing from 20th Sept. to 1st Oct. Harvest can be much later than in table. *Note* Successively later sowing takes longer to produce due to waning light.	Important to give a 'warm' start. Average temp. as above. Ventilate at 65°–68°F (18–20°C), warmer for CO_2. Ventilate more freely when heating commences to avoid looseness.	A difficult crop in poor light areas or bad seasons. Glassiness (see page 106) (a form of *Oedema*) is a hazard due to high humidity as is disease loss. If quality good prices high.
'Early spring' mildly heated. *Note* Seed sown in batches of 7 days.	As per table. Sowing from 10th Oct. to 20th Oct. Here again there can be harvest delay.	As low as 40°F (4–5°C) night, 45°F (7°C) day but will gradually rise in Feb./March. Ventilation on scale 65–68°F (18–20°C)	As above but with improving light disease risk less. Prices variable.
'Spring' heated initially to rosette stage then grown relatively cool with frost protection. *Note* Seed sown in batches of 7 days.	As per table. Sowing from 1st Nov. to 27th Feb. Harvesting fairly predictable.	40°F (45°C) – 45°F (7°C) temperatures satisfactory in winter – rising gradually as above but 'cooling off' before harvesting. Ventilate generally in middle of day if plants are soft.	Can be 'glut' periods with poor prices.
'Summer' Successional sowings. *Note* Intervals of 2–4 days between batches.	As per table. Sowing over periods planting 14–21 days later; harvesting is as little as 50–55 days in best conditions.	Critical care required, ventilation and watering.	For high quality continuous lettuce, marketing prices can vary widely, and depend much on quality and presentation.

Systems of Propagation

Method 1	Quantity	Procedures	Comments
Natural seed in boxes into blocks or paper pots. Research is proceeding into direct sowing of natural seed into blocks, using specialized 'sowing' equipment.	$1/3$–$1/2$ g, 250–400 seeds per box well spaced	Seed thinly in peat or John Innes seed composts. Pricked off into blocks (4.3–7.5 cm) or paper pots $1\frac{1}{2}$–2 in (3.8–5 cm) containing good compost.* Seedlings can be 'lit' for 72 hours continuously before pricking off. *Lower nitrogen for winter, see Chapter 17.	High labour costs. Checks to seedlings inevitable. Free draining compost essential to encourage root growth.

Lettuce Under Glass or Plastic 95

Method 2	Quantity	Procedures	Comments
Natural seed in boxes, borders or frames. Research is proceeding into direct sowing of natural seed into blocks using specialized 'sowing' equipment.	¼–⅓ g per box, 200 seeds or 1 g/m² in border or frames in sterilized soil.	Seed pricked off direct to growing borders.	Still greater checks to planting and chance of disease risk. Lack of uniformity will affect harvesting.

Method 3			
Pelleted (split pill) seed with automatic block machine.	Seeds sold by number (see page 92); topping up of 'misses' necessary. Blocking output variable. 4.3 cm block size ideal. (see notes on germination).	Blocks 'collected' on waxed hardboard or mica sheets of a size to avoid gaps. Lighting necessary in poor light areas in winter. See also No. 1 above as compromise may be desirable.	The 'ideal' system with good blocking compost in good light areas. Light treatments overcome propagating difficulties but poor natural light will slow up 'programmes' (see page 93). Strict attention to hygiene necessary to avoid disease and infection.

Method 4			
Pelleted seed using hand blocking machine placing in pellets or pills by hand.	Seeds sold by number	See Method 3.	Good system for small grower. Labour content higher, capital investment less.

Composts for Propagation

Reference is made to compost formulation in Chapter 17.
  The important issues are:–
1 pH of compost – whether peat- or soil-based.
  A pH of 6.5 for soil-based composts.
  A pH of 5.5–5.8 for peat-based composts.
2 Seed sowing composts, peat/sand, or soil containing use low level nutrients for winter sowing (low level of nitrogen especially).
3 Higher level of nutrients for spring/summer for seed sowing and potting, especially nitrogen.
4 Blocking composts are usually made up with peat and no sand plus some sterilized soil for binding if required. Many growers buy in their blocking composts, including Dutch Polder Soil.
5 Freedom from pests and diseases.
It is the author's experience that it is dangerous to be too categorical about compost mixture. Raw materials and bought compost vary and practical experience goes a long way.

96 Lettuce Under Glass or Plastic

Growing Room Raising for Lettuce
Various techniques are involved – but basically are as follows:
Seed is germinated in germinating cabinets or 'stacked' at 62°F (16°C). New chemicals are being introduced into pellet to avoid high-temperature dormancy.

Avoiding high temperatures:
Where pricking out is involved light is given 3 days at 8,000 lx for 24 hours after germination in tiered room or 15,000 lx on 12 hour batch basis in linear room, or bench lighting and thereafter (after pricking out) 8 days on the same basis as above. For direct sown block lettuce, give 11 days as above. Temperatures during light treatment are:
    68°F (20°C) for 24 hours lighting
    70°F (21°C) unlit and 75°F (24°C) lit for batch treatment.

Nutritional Standards (A.D.A.S.)

Under Protected Culture

Optimal pH 6.5–7	Summer	Winter
Nitrogen – Index 1–2 (ideally)	N.100 ppm (mg/litre) in soil	Less 20–30% of summer levels
Phosphorus – Index 5–6	P.71–140 ppm (mg/litre)	
Potash – Index 3–4	K.245–600 ppm (mg/litre)	
Magnesium 2–3	Mg 51–175 ppm (mg/litre)	
(Potash/Magnesium ratio 3–1) Salt Content Low Index 2	Lettuce does not like high salt content	

Nutrient levels can be adjusted in several ways following soil analysis.
(1) Application of lime to adjust pH.
(2) By individual adjustment of N.P.K. as advised by analytical body.

Nitrogen – Ammonium nitrate: ½ oz sq yd (17 g/m^2) will result in an index change of 1 digit (approx.).

Phosphorus: Triple superphosphates 1 oz per sq yd (34 g/m^2) will result in index change of 1 digit (approx.).

Potash: Sulphate of potash 1 oz per sq yd (34 g/m^2) will result in an index change of 1 digit (very approx.).

(3) Application of base feed normally 'medium' potash (9-9-13) evenly applied and tilled into top 9 in (22 cm) of soil 3–4 oz per sq yd (100–135 g/m^2) plus 1 oz (34 g/m^2) of ammonium nitrate for spring/ summer crops only. Often base feeds can be ignored especially following steam sterilization and farmyard manure (FYM) has been applied but it is always advisable to have soils checked by analysis *especially for high salt content* and to avoid very high fertility levels in winter. (Flood to reduce high salt content.)

Weed Control

It is not usual practice to apply weedkillers under protected cultivation, soil preferably being sterilized by heat or chemicals. Weedkillers such as Paraquat can be used (various brands) before planting where soil is prepared in advance. The chemical Chlorpropham can be used according to directions.

Careful weed control may be necessary outside the structure as weeds can be a constant source of trouble, introducing pests and diseases.

Preparation for Crop

Avoidance of Disease

Where border cropping is concerned some form of soil sterilization, usually sheet steaming with steam, is advisable. Houses should also be thoroughly cleaned down. While chemicals can be used these can involve a waiting period and this is not always desirable, although Methyl Bromide is very useful. Before planting it is advisable to use Quintozene dust (Botrilex), against *rhizoctonia* (root rot), and other soil-borne problems at 1 oz per sq yd (34 g/m^2). Dichloran (Allisan) can be used as a preventative against *botrytis* – but sprays on the actual crop are highly effective using Benomyl (Benlate), Dichlofluanid (Elvaron), or Iprodione (Rovral) sprays, especially during winter production in humid or moist areas. Metaxanine (Ridomil) may also be used against mildew (*bremia*).

It is essential to avoid careless handling or deep planting, especially for winter crops – as this quickly predisposes plants to *botrytis*.

Lettuce on Nutrient Film Technique

Lettuce may now be grown on sloping beds using N.F.T. systems (see Chapter 15).

Ground Preparation

Good cultivation methods are essential for lettuce crops. If available, well-rotted farmyard manure should be incorporated at 30–40 tons per acre (31–41 tonnes). Farmyard manure must be 'clean', otherwise it can create a tremendous weed problem. Alternatively, and with less weed problems if the structure of the soil is poor because the organic matter is low, peat can be used at varying amounts according to organic matter levels, generally around 5 tons/acre (12 tonnes/ha). Note that if a lot of peat is used this will lower the pH of the soil. The main benefit of high organic matter content is moisture conservation. Cultivation of ground to 9 in depth (22 cm) and incorporation of fertilizers is usually carried out by rotary cultivation, although care should be taken to avoid panning of the sub-soil and, if this is in evidence, sub-soiling will be required.

Following cultivation, firming up the ground is necessary by rolling or on a small scale with feet. Soil analysis is an essential prelude to all cultivations to check whether the ground needs fertilizers or flooding to lower soluble salt content. If watering or flooding is necessary this is done with spray lines sufficiently in advance of planting to allow the ground to dry out and be worked to a good tilth. For nutritional standards see page 96, which gives details concerning liming and base feeds. These if possible should be applied a week before planting and cultivated or flooded in.

Crop Raising (Refer to Tables, pages 93 and 94)

Where bare seed is used this is generally sown in boxes 250–400 seeds per standard seed tray which is approximately $1/3$–$1/2$ g seed. The seed should be sown in John Innes seed or appropriate soilless compost and covered lightly. The boxes are well watered and stacked, being covered with polythene. The optimum germination temperature is 62°F (16°C) but seeds will germinate at both lower and higher temperatures. The seed may be difficult to germinate if too fresh and generally up to six months is necessary for the seed to mature. To break dormancy, seed can be spread on wet blotting paper and given around 40°F (4.4°C) for 48 hours in a refrigerator, when it is then sown and germinated below 60°F (16°C). Seed can also be sown and then cold treated if such facilities are available (cold room). Seed may also not germinate if temperatures are too high (above 80°F/27°C) which involves selecting a shaded area or keeping the seed boxes or blocks cool by shading with polystyrene, sowing the seed in the evening and damping well. *Note also that short days, by blacking out to give a 10-hour day, are necessary for short-day varieties sown before August 21st (U.K.).* Successive cropping involves as quick a turn round as possible going through the same basic procedures, although note that sterilization of border soil is not generally needed between all crops. A few growers still sow lettuce seed in shallow drills in greenhouse borders and they can also be sown broadcast approximately 1 g seed per sq metre. This procedure was very popular in the

East Riding of Yorkshire. If seed was sown thinly enough the seedlings could be allowed to make good development before transplanting. Where the seedlings have to be handled directly out of seed boxes there is a limit as to how long they can be left and checks are inevitable. In all cases seed must be given as much light as possible once germinated.

Germination of pelleted seed in any form is best effected by seed being on the surface, sprayed lightly to encourage germination.

Sowing Pelleted Seeds in Peat/Blocks*

(Information by Dutch seed merchants.)

The optimum conditions for lettuce pill germination are temperatures of 59–68°F (15–20°C) and a relative atmospheric humidity in excess of 70% throughout the whole of the germination period.

High temperatures during spring/summer are a hazard to germination, particularly during the period June to September. To obtain satisfactory germination certain precautionary measures are necessary.

Official research in the Netherlands supported by large-scale practical trials has led to the following advice in order to obtain the best possible germination when conditions are extremely warm and dry.

1. Shade the propagation house at least one week before sowing and always keep the floor (soil or concrete) wet before sowing. Ventilate freely at all times.
2. Do not commence sowing until after 1800 hours.
3. Immediately after sowing spray the blocks liberally together with the propagation house structure, walls, roof, pathways etc., by means of a high pressure machine, capable of achieving a mist spray effect. Do not cover with polystyrene sheeting on this or any subsequent night-time.
4. The following morning before sunrise, mist spray the soil blocks prior to covering with polystyrene sheeting, then spray over the polystyrene sheeting together with all the surfaces in the propagation house as before. Ventilators must be kept fully open.
5. During the course of the day mist spray periodically over the polystyrene sheeting along with all the surfaces in the propagation house keeping them moist at all times. The frequency of this operation will vary dependent upon the prevailing temperature; however, the atmosphere must always 'smell' fresh.
6. In the evening after 2000 hours remove the polystyrene sheets and mist spray over the soil blocks and propagation house structure, etc.
7. Repeat as per items 4, 5 and 6 daily until germination takes place.

On a smaller scale seedlings can be pricked off into small peat pots containing a good compost (John Innes No. 2 or soilless) but this is considered too labour intensive in light of direct block sowing. It is also

100 Lettuce Under Glass or Plastic

claimed that the checks to plant growth which result would affect the final quality of the product.

Very considerable experimentation has been carried out over the years to find not only suitable containers but type and quality of growing media or substrate which not only provides a good balance and reserve of nutrients but gives a good air/moisture relationship. Where pots are used paper or peat types varied in size from 1½–2 in (3.8–5 cm) are popular and they may be filled with a range of composts but it is important to note the labour requirement, which is critical. General trends are certainly into peat blocks (see Chapter 17) or direct sowing in paper pots with proprietary peat compost. Note the output of blocks per hour for different size blocking machine varies.

Normal block size for self-propagation is the 7.5 cm block; for 'buying in' 4.3 cm blocks.

Large-scale Plant Propagation

Several companies in the U.K. and on the Continent specialize in large-scale plant propagation for sale to growers. One such in the U.K. is 'Crystal Heart' in Humberside (near Hull). They claim that specialized propagation is much more economically viable to the grower than 'home' propagation – and that better, more reliable, pest-and-disease-free (plants are treated) plants are available. This is a matter which each grower must evaluate.

Lettuce is produced for sale by 'Crystal Heart' in 4.3 cm peat blocks. They are delivered in stacking returnable trays each weighing 30 lbs (13.6 kg) measuring 26½ in (67.3 cm) × 17½ in (44.5 cm) × 4 ³⁄₈ in (approx. 11 cm) deep, stacked 18 in high when full (holding 140 blocks). To work out whether purchase of plants is viable, take into account the capital investment, returns, labour, fuel cost, and last but by no means least, waste on 'home' propagation.

Planting

Planting procedures for setting out the plants vary enormously but generally it is advised that the plants should be at the 4–5 leaf stage. For medium/large-scale planting longitudinal rows are etched on the ground with a marking board or marking roller, transverse lines can be best done with a kneeling board under which canes are attached at the appropriate distance apart so that during the planting procedure the ground is automatically marked. Plants can be set out with small dibbers or trowels either by hand or preferably by planting machines of the indent kind. This reduces the labour content very considerably.

After planting it is advisable to mist spray and keep the ventilation

Lettuce Under Glass or Plastic

limited and thereafter allow the plants to establish until they have a reasonable leaf spread when they can be watered and ventilated on a regular basis according to temperature, soil type, etc.

Spacing the Crop

Various experiments to determine ideal spacing for lettuce have been carried out over many years. Varieties vary in size but an average planting distance is around 8 × 8 in or 8 × 9 (20 × 20 × 20 in or 22.5 cm). This gives a plant density of 58,000 – 65,000 per acre *planted* (143,300–160,600 ha) but here again local experience is valuable.

Temperatures

In general lettuce respond to low night, high day regimes (see page 94), effectively controlled especially where carbon dioxide enrichment is practised (see below).

Ventilation is freely carried out to avoid high day temperatures which means more careful ventilation during day periods between spring and autumn but avoiding drastic changes (see page 106).

Watering

It is difficult to state water requirements with any great degree of accuracy. Water is generally supplied by overhead irrigation. Plants are set out in moist soil, it having been given water to field capacity according to soil type. Soil peat blocks on the surface (indent planting) must not be allowed to dry out, therefore light dampings are given to keep surface moist and avoid restricting root growth by water logging. 'Normal' quantities of water throughout the full season are very variable.

Carbon Dioxide Enrichment

Research at the Glasshouse Crops Research Institute, Littlehampton, has shown the value of carbon dioxide enrichment at 800–1,000 vpm continuously from the post-rosette stage in good light conditions. The net effect is to produce better quality, heavier lettuce more quickly, which realizes higher prices.

It is stressed that glasshouses must be tight to avoid leakage of the CO_2.

The purity of the CO_2 is also important, avoiding the contamination of some direct-fired paraffin burners, which will tend to nullify the benefit of the carbon dioxide.

Seasonal Procedures

Very careful watch must be made on crop with particular emphasis on watering, ventilation and spraying with fungicides if necessary (see page 105).

Marketing
It is usual to cut and pack lettuce within the glasshouse area and one worker can pack 18–20 boxes per hour, 7000 boxes per acre for a manhour input of 350 hours.

Lettuce are graded, checked and marketed in polythene bags in single layer cardboard trays. The marketing situation is a changing one and 'point of sale' growing lettuce (a form of N.F.T.) is a technique which is likely to develop.

Harvesting 'machines' are available which reduce cutting labour but these can cause crop damage and demand capital investment.

Palletization is useful to remove lettuce to a cool place as soon as possible – before grading according to laid down standards, if this has not already been done within the glasshouse area.

Lettuce in Plastic Structures
Techniques and procedures are basically similar to culture under glass with the exception that crops are invariably grown 'cold'. Humidities being higher in tunnels necessitates much more vigilance with ventilation and watering. Keep a sharp lookout for outbreaks of *botrytis*; make careful choice of varieties. Normally regular 'fogging' with fungicides is advisable.

Lettuce in Frames, Cloches and Film Material
The high labour aspects of frame culture throws some doubt on economic viability and the same may be said of cloches. Undoubtedly however, frames and cloches have a role and are useful for limited areas of production on smaller units. Cultural techniques are broadly similar. The more recent use of perforated film material has much application for lettuce growing.

Mobile Glasshouses and Intercropping Techniques
The ability to 'de-cover' crops of lettuce to mature out of doors and start another crop of lettuce or other items on a rotation basis was thought to be highly advantageous at one time, especially in the 1950s. Now with low cost plastic cover it is doubtful economically yet from the strict angle of investment and return there is still virtue in considering mobiles. This enthusiasm has not been greatly shared among growers in recent years. The same is true of intercropping techniques. The following is a typical example:

Plot one	Plot two	Plot three
Lettuce sown in heat, planted Feb/March Lettuce planted Sept. covered Oct/Nov.	Lettuce de-covered April – Planted with tomatoes new site	Mid season chrysanthemums planted May/June, covered Sept.

Lettuce Under Glass or Plastic

Intercropping techniques are possible using lettuce combined with radish, dahlias or gladioli.

Crop Economics

Crop Definition
Year round
Highest price periods – Spring – October/November
Packed in boxes of 12 (Class 1)

Average Actual Yields, allowing for cropping loss

Summer/Autumn	Winter/Spring
13–14 sq yd	15–16 sq yd
16–17 m²	19–20 m²

Costs

sq yd	m²
Compost (blocks) .13 cu ft (or plants bought in at actual cost)	3.5 litres (or plants bought in at cost)
Manure (FYM) *Not* for every crop. Usually *once* per year 15 lb	7 kg
Fertilizers *average* per crop 2–3 oz	68–102 g
Sterilants Methyl Bromide .1 lb	.45 kg
Sprays – 1% of gross revenue	Sprays – 1% of gross revenue
Water – very variable up to 22 gal	up to 100 litres
* Fuel (Oil) Nil in spring/early autumn up to 1–2 gal (or more) according to region and season	5–10 litres
Seed Pelleted 15–16 pellets	22–22 pellets

* Plus CO_2 costs if used

Marketing Costs = 12–14% of gross income

Labour Units
1 man hour per 3–4 sq yd
1 man hour per 3–3.5 m²

Lettuce Pest and Disease Check
There are three main aspects of pest and disease control.
1. The utmost hygiene at the outset – and precision with fertilizers, watering, etc. Avoidance of careless handling or mechanical damage on planting.
2. Preventive measures by means of regular sprays or dusts.
3. Quick action should a specific trouble occur – calling in, if necessary, an adviser or consultant – who can if need be seek specialist help.

The chemical situation is also a changing one.

104 Lettuce Under Glass or Plastic

Pests

Problem	Symptoms	Control if any
Slugs	Leaves eaten.	Slug Bait Methiocarb (Draza) well distributed at 5 lb per acre 2 kg/ha. Metaldehyde suspension can also be used.
Mice	Eating plants.	Extensive trapping and baiting with various materials, Warfarin, Coumatetralyl, etc.
Birds	Pluck out seedlings especially from pellets.	Exclude by nettting – treat bare seed with red lead or less dangerously with Anthroquinone.
Aphids, many species especially lettuce aphid which can attack all year, *Nasonaria ribisnigri*	Blistering distortion of leaves (Virus also spread see page 105).	Spray on a routine basis with various chemicals e.g. Dimethoate (Rogor E) Formothion (Anthio) etc. noting clearance period before harvesting.
Cutworms, Caterpillars of various species of moth	Plants eaten off at ground level. Grey grubs 1 in (2.5 cm) can be found in area of plants.	Localized hand killing effective in bad areas. Preventive sprays before or after planting or sprays of organophosphorus materials. Malathion Mevinphos Dichlorvos to try and kill grubs.
Wireworms	Common on 'new' land – ploughed from turf larvae burrow into stems.	Use Gamma HCH in either dust or spray form if attack suspected or confirmed. Normally soil sterilization is fully effective.
Lettuce root maggot (*Psila nigricornis*)	Yellow grub ¼ in (75 mm) long which evacuates root core.	As for wireworms use Gamma HCH.
Symphilids *Scutigerella immaculata*	White centipede-like insects congregate on root hairs causing wilting and general lack of growth. (They will float to surface in a bucket of water.) Disease may follow as secondary issue.	Use Parathion or Diazinon drenches observing harvesting clearance time.
Eeelworm *Meloidogyne spp.* (resistant races have developed due to widespread use of organophosphorus chemicals – especially in warm countries)	Swellings on roots. Plants pale and wilt.	Soil sterilization with steam or chemicals including 'DD' (which can persist in heavy soils).
Lettuce root aphid (*Pemphigus busarius*)	Clusters of white aphids like cotton wool on roots which may restrict growth in large numbers.	Use Gamma HCH dust or drench with Malathion or Diazinon (note clearance time).
Millipedes	Long snakelike insects only damaging if in large numbers.	Gamma HCH dust or drenches.

Lettuce Under Glass or Plastic

Diseases

Problem	Symptoms	Control if any
Botrytis Grey mould *Botrytis cinerea*	Widespread damage to leaves and stems preceded by wilting – when fungus attacks stems at soil level.	Good growing methods/good in theory but difficult in practice due to outside weather influence. Water in morning only; sterilize between crops with Formaldehyde. It is normal to use PCNB (Quintozene) and Dicloran (Allisan) dust at 1 oz/sq yd (34 g/m^2) before planting as a routine measure against *rhizocotonia* and *botrytis*, and follow this with dust or spray of 'fogging' during the season using a variety of chemicals chiefly Elvaron, (Dichlofluanid) Benomyl (Benlate) or Iprodine (Rovral).
Downy mildew, *Bremia lactucae*, several different races	Areas of leaves attacked by white fluffy growth under light green areas. Common in autumn/winter when humidity high.	Grow resistant varieties (note at least three different races of disease). Spray regularly with fungicides Zineb etc. Good cover of crop is essential.
Rhizocotonia solani (Collar rot)	Seedlings topple at ground level – also rotting at base of mature plants. Secondary infection with *botrytis* likely.	Good hygiene for seedlings. Pre-dust with Quintozene noting that in high temperatures damage can occur so keep rate low. In Holland Combison is used – this being a mixture of Quintozene and Dicloran.
Pythium	Seedlings affected, damping off.	Avoid sowing too thickly; use sterilized soil or clean compost.
Other troubles Black root rot, *thielaviopsis basicola*	Plants wilt and die.	Not common in sterilized soil or soilless compost.
Sclerotinia sclerotiorum	A warm weather disease appears before cutting. Black fruiting bodies distinctive.	Spray with Benomyl (Benlate).

Virus Diseases

There are three main viruses, with others occurring occasionally.

Mosiac Spread by seed and aphids especially peach potato aphid	Mottling and stunting of growth.	Buy as 'clean' seed as possible. Destroy badly affected plants quickly. Control aphids with systemic insecticides.
Cucumber Mosaic Spread by aphids from many plants especially chickweed	As above but plants generally more yellow with leaf spotting.	Destroy affected plants. Control aphids.
Big Vein Spread by the fungus *olpidium*	Broadening of veins – with light green borders.	Not crippling; practise good culture with special attention to hygiene.

106 Lettuce Under Glass or Plastic

Physiological and Chemical Disorders

Tipburn Takes two forms: outer and older leaves or leaves around heart	Layer of dead cells caused by too rapid moisture loss.	Caused by irregularities of any kind. Avoid drying out. Ventilate early in morning and avoid excess salt concentrations.
Glassiness or Veinal Tipburn, a form of *oedema*	Plants unable to lose moisture quickly enough due to high humidity.	Worst in dull humid weather. Keep up temperatures *with* ventilation to lower humidity.
Low temperature damage	Takes several forms, generally a browning of foliage.	Avoid too low temperatures if practical to do so.

Nutritional Deficiencies and Upsets.

See Chapter 16 on nutritional problems.

Chapter Fourteen

Other Vegetables

The author stresses the lack of *total* information on 'less important' crops. See Lee Valley Effort and Stockbridge House E.H.S. Annual Reports. *Note:* Seed firms are listed in the Appendix.

Aubergine (Egg Plant)

Solanum melongena, various varieties, approx. 220 seeds per g.

Introduction
The egg plant is a member of the tomato family, to which peppers also belong. It is a bushy plant which in warm climates (probably a native of India) grows to a height of 5–6 ft having a fruit 12–15 in (30–37½ cm) long. There are dwarf forms having pear-shaped small fruits and these are best adapted to areas of shorter growing season. Modern varieties tend to be a hybrid between the 'tall' and dwarf forms. While demand for egg plant fruits is increasing in the U.K., market survey is advisable before becoming involved in large-scale growing projects. There is a good outlet selling plants to amateur gardeners.

Culture
Basically speaking culture is the same as tomatoes, seed being sown in boxes at 65°F (18°C) 8–10 weeks prior to 'planting out' in borders or pots. Aubergines are subject to the same monocultural problems as tomatoes if they are to crop well – which may mean the adoption of grow bags, straw bales, or on a smaller scale pots – 9 in (22 cm) whale hides (with bottoms) being a convenient unit. They dislike growth checks. For early crops seedlings (unpricked off) will respond to 5 days of artificial light at 15,000 lx for 24 or 12 hours at 70°F (21°C) unlit – 77°F (25°C) lit. The same applies to plants after pricking off if light

108 Other Vegetables

levels are poor – although longer periods of lighting can be given. For later sown crops (into March) lighting is unnecessary.

Plant treatment during the propagation period is similar to tomatoes – with potting composts also similar (see Chapter 17). Spacing plants out well during propagation is important, as also is *overwatering* – especially if peat composts are used.

Planting

Nutritional levels are similar to tomatoes, pH 6–6.5 with P.K. mg indexes around 4, but susceptibility of aubergines (and peppers) to high salt levels has been noted by many growers (see tomatoes).

If growing in pots aim at J.I.P. 2 level – which means if using soil-less composts adding *medium* levels of fertilizer.

Plants can be grown on straw bales – but note the danger of high salt levels.

Spacing in Growing Quarters

This will depend on house width, but in wider spans, double rows 18 in (45 cm) at 5 ft centres (150 cm) is usual – plants being 15 in (38 cm) apart in the row.

In narrow houses (or tunnels) planting 18 in square (45 cm) is usually more convenient.

Pot grown plants are best set out at 18 in (45 cm) centres. Where a few plants are grown on benches following propagation, spacing is not critical.

Training

Plants are supported with vertical strings or canes – and also with horizontal ties or loops around the plants to keep them from sprawling if 2–3 stems are allowed to develop.

How much plant pruning to do is a matter of some difference of opinion – to avoid overcropping. While 2–3 stems may be taken, plants can be maintained on one stem with side shoots reduced beyond the flowers which form. The basic object is to aim to take 8–12 fruits per plant, although this can certainly be exceeded considerably on longer term culture, and experience with varieties and growing systems is necessary before being too categoric. Lower leaves are removed when senescent (yellowing) as they will trail and become diseased.

Temperatures

There is evidence of poor setting of fruit if night temperatures are too high – and as high humidity is also said to encourage poor setting this can pose management problems. Ideally the plants seem to respond to high day/lower night temperatures, the aim being, as stated, to produce

Other Vegetables

8–12 fruits per plant and yields below and above this will depend much on the length of growing season, variety and several other factors. Broadly speaking, it is a crop where a little growing experience goes a long way and so far in the U.K. there has not been a lot of research, although information on peppers is broadly applicable.

Feeding and Watering
Basically similar to tomatoes, with more emphasis on nitrogen to encourage and maintain growth, noting the danger of high salt build up which will cause fruit blotching and sunken areas.

Troubles
Basically similar to tomatoes – with physiological problems more likely to develop due to a combination of high humidity and high salts.

Marketing
Fruit must be carefully packed in single layers to avoid bruising.

Economics
Broadly similar to tomatoes – yields lower but prices higher. From 25 ton/acre – 23 lb/sq yd (62 tonne/ha – 6.2 kg/m^2) up to 50 ton/acre – 46 lbs/sq yd (125 tonne/ha – 12.5 kg/m^2 under best long-term growing conditions.

It is *not* a crop which should be developed too quickly until marketing demands are assessed.

Labour units variable, similar to tomatoes.

Pests and Disease Check
See tomatoes.

Beans, Dwarf French

Seed count 20–40 seeds per 10 g.
Seed requirement – 30–40 kg per acre (67–100 kg/ha).

Limited demand for cold glass/polythene protected crop but yields too low to be really attractive. Seed can be sown in paper/peat pots, or soil/peat blocks in *mild* heat for planting in unheated plastic glass or cloches – but careful timing is advisable to avoid frost risk. Plant out 6–8 in (15–20 cm) apart in rows 16–20 in (40–50 cm) apart. In general it is safer and less labour-demanding to sow in situ 2–3 weeks in advance of outside sowing (e.g. 3rd week of April in South of England). Sow seeds 2 in (5 cm) deep 5 per foot (15/m) in rows 16–20 in (40–50 cm) apart.

Other Vegetables

Soil should have pH 6.5–7 N.P.K. index of 2–3 and be dressed with a 10–10–10 fertilizer at 2 oz per sq yd (68 g/m^2). Avoid rapid temperature and water variations which will interfere with setting. Market in cardboard boxes containing approx. 8 lb (3–4 kg).

Economics
Yields vary enormously but a 'target' should be in the region of 1–2 lb/sq yd (0.5–1 kg/m^2) which puts them in a poor light when compared to other crops – and would require to be part of a rotation to make the use of protection viable. Labour units are low however at 1 man hour per 8–10 sq yd (6.5–8m^2).

Pest and Disease Check
See runner beans.

Beans, Runner

Seed count approx 10 per 10 g.

A crop which has been shown in trials and practice to have a lot of potential outdoors. Basically speaking it is not a crop to 'risk' under protection except in cool districts in view of the high yield potential of the outdoor crop raised in peat/plastic pots and planted out when frost risk is past. Note the allowance of plenty of space for the crop, generally 18 in (45 cm) spacing on single plants per cane or string. Yields of over 12 ton/acre (30 tonne/ha) are regularly recorded outdoors.

Beans, Climbing French

Seed count approx. 20–30 per 10 g.
Seed requirement 20–30/acre (50–70 kg/ha).

These offer greater scope for profit than Dwarf French Beans but have a higher labour demand as a support system is involved.

Seed Raising
Soil conditions and sowing time are similar to Dwarf French, but the greater yields make use of *mild* heat feasible – bringing forward the sowing dates – bearing in mind that *frost protection is essential*. Heat can be conserved by sowing seeds in 3½ in (9 cm) peat pots in mild warmth and timing both sowing and eventual planting in structures until frost risk is past – as planting out should not be delayed unduly to avoid

checks to growth. Spacing trials at Lee Valley E.H.S. indicate single rows in preference to the usual double rows – to let more light into the crop. Space plants in double rows 6 in (15 cm) apart or single rows at 18 in – 2 ft centres, suitably spaced to allow a 3 ft path access. Support on strings or high nets, pinching plants out at top, and be very vigilant of ventilation as stress will cause bud drop. Density trials with the bean family generally have shown the value of adequate spacing which much improves the yield.

Economics

Not a great deal of really accurate data available, but target yields should be up to 3–4 lb/sq yd (1.5–2 kg/m^2) or higher. Direct costs approximately 30% of gross income to which must be added labour – 1 man hour per 10–12 sq yd (8–10m^2) estimate.

Pests and Disease Check for Beans

Aphis – distorted foliage. Use range of insecticides.
Foot rot (*Fusarium sp*). Rotate crop, or sterilize.
French fly – a mite which causes holes in foliage. Frequently carried on straw. Use range of insecticides.
Red spider mite – speckled leaves. Spray with water. Use range of insecticides but observe clearance time.
Halo blight – a bacterial problem often caused by overhead watering. Obtain resistant varieties.
Anthracnose – dark spots on leaves stems and pods. No effective control – but buy reliable seed.
Botrytis – blackening of stems, leaves and pods. Avoid high humidities and spray with fungicide on regular basis.
Flower dropping – avoid irregularities of temperature and water as far as practical. Mulching the soil helps.

Beetroot (Beta vulgaris)

Seed count 400–1500 per 10 g. (variable). This is not a vegetable grown a great deal under glass or plastic, but it does give reasonable results for an early crop as a bunched beet.

Soil need only be of moderate fertility level, pH 6–6.5, soil index P:K 2–3.

Do not sow too early (late March/April), otherwise there are problems of day length and the effect of low temperatures on young plants. Sow seeds either broadcast and firmed in with the feet, or in drills 12 in (30 cm) apart.

Give adequate watering and free ventilation in spring months.

Economics
Target yield of 4–5 lb/sq yd (2–3 kg/m²).
Labour units 1 man hour per 14–16 sq yd (15 m²).

Pest and Disease Check
Look out for damping off, flea beetle and 'bolting' due to a combination of early sowing and growth checks due to dryness.

Brassicas

Seed count 2,500–4,500 per 10 g.

Brassicas, including cabbage, cauliflowers, calabrese, sprouting and heading broccoli and brussels sprouts can be produced with advantage to be sold to growers or amateurs under glass or plastic in cold districts for eventual planting outside. Some such as cauliflower and calabrese can also be grown as an unheated crop under protection – especially early cauliflowers. Early and late calabrese to extend the season can be very useful for direct selling to a retail outlet or in a farm shop to act as inducement to customers.

Early varieties and late varieties are selected, and preferably block grown – being planted at a suitable time for region both early and late. Much work is in process at the Lee Valley E.H.S., Hertfordshire, in this whole area of 'alternative' crops.

Sow brassicas 30–50 days before required for planting out of doors thinly in boxes, or seed trays – individually in small peat pots or 4.3 cm peat blocks or multi-seeded (3 seeds per 7.5 cm block of pointed spring and early summer cabbage – the same for calabrese and broccoli).

Early cauliflower is more successful with less 'buttoning' in 7.5 cm blocks. Use soil with John Innes No. 1 standard or soilless peat of high pH6. Sow by hand or using blocking/seeding machines (pelleted seed). Lighting for early cauliflower at 15,000 lx for 12–16 hours per day up to 14 days is helpful (*watch* temperatures). As soon as possible after germination give adequate ventilation. Standard practice is to sow directly in cold frames in March, April or October, trying to space seed thinly broadcast or in drills 6 in (15 cm) apart. Cauliflower however can be grown to maturity under cold glass, planted at 2 × 2 ft (60 × 60 cm) apart intercropped with lettuce. Look out for club root and blackleg especially in compost or frame soil. Dressed seed is essential.

Economics
Supply of plants for sale can be lucrative especially direct to retail customers. Whether they are prepared to pay for block-raised plants

Other Vegetables

will depend on region involved. It is a mistake to have plants ready *too early*.

For cauliflower under glass rotation is necessary to make the protected area viable, following with lettuce, marrows or other crops. Bear in mind that cauliflower from early districts may clash with the early crop under protection in a later area.

Carrots (Daucus carota)

Seed count variable 5,000 – 16,000 per 10 g.

Stump-rooted types give delicious early salad crops under glass as bunched crop.

Preparation
Good greenhouse weed-free border soil, well dug and firmed, pH 6.5–6, soil index N.P.K. 1.3.3 (Mg–1). General fertilizer 6:6:10–12. Sow broadcast seed 1/28th oz sq yd ($\frac{1}{4}$ g/m^2) or in drills 6 in (15 cm) apart. Firm down with a spade. Allow for 60–70% germination, late January/February/March.

Cultivation
Little thinning required. Attend to watering and ventilation.

Pest and Disease Check
Nothing of consequence, as the crop is usually too early for carrot fly attack (Gamma H.C.H. dust). Beware of bolting due to growth checks (especially with early sowings).

Celery, Self-Blanching

Seed count approx. 30,000 per 10 g.

A crop of excellent potential for cold protected areas, frames, cold glass, plastics – both for early summer and late autumn harvest. (There is much scope for the block-raised plants for the whole range of celery crop.)

Seed Sowing
Celery may be raised in a variety of ways – and methods are changing. It is important to avoid sowing too early in year – owing to the risk of 'bolting' (a day length response).

Early Crop
Sow in sterilized soil or soilless compost, in boxes around February until mid March for early crops or later for autumn crops. Good clean compost is essential as celery is very prone to seedling troubles. Seed dressings/plus Thiram soaking carried out by seed firms is very effective in avoiding trouble. Sow thinly, pressing seed into surface and subsequently prick off 40 per seed tray in JIP or soilless or into soil/peat blocks. Direct sowing into peat blocks using mini-pellet seed is now developed and further techniques are being experimented with including fluid drilling. The small nature of celery seed, and its generally low percentage germination makes it a difficult seed to sow individually unless by special methods. Avoidance of checks to growth – including root damage (plants rooting out of block into bench or borders) — is an essential part of seedling production. Ideally celery seedlings are best produced in peat blocks on concrete floors or polythene sheets to avoid extraneous rooting and for hygienic reasons.

Germinate at not less than 60°F (15°C) and reduce to 55°F (13°C) after germination to avoid soft disease-prone growth. Seedlings respond to lighting at 15,000 lx for 12 hours for up to 15 days.

Preparation for Planting
Celery loves moist organic soil. The use of spent mushroom compost or peat is good practice. Adjust the pH to around 5.5–6 and N.P.K. index of 1.4.3. If required (following analysis) base fertilizer is applied. Use a balanced type 10–8–10 at up to 4 oz sq yd ($136g/m^2$), and produce a good tilth on planting surface.

Planting
Plants are spaced at from 9 × 9 in (22.5 × 22.5 cm) to 10 × 10 in (25 × 25 cm) with similar planting methods to lettuce. Firm planting is essential. Note the risk of frost under plastic especially. Water in the plants well and feed if necessary with high nitrogen feed (see page 163). When established, weed control may be necessary using Prometryne or similar weedkiller.

Late Crop
Sow late June, for planting mid August to harvest in November/December *but note that effective frost control will be required to avoid serious crop damage.*

Marketing
Crop is pulled when ready (even sized with good 'blanch'), graded and polythene sleeved. It must be clean and attractively presented in non-returnable cardboard trays or suitable containers.

Economics

At plant densities of 12–16 sq yd (14–19 m^2) and high percentage cut, output is not difficult to assess bearing in mind fluctuating markets and vast price differences around the country. Note also imports from many warm countries (including the U.S.A.) from where the crop is transported in cool containers. Marketing costs are likely to be 12–15% of gross. Input for fuel is not high and seed costs are low (around 10 g of seed per 15,000 plants).

Main cost is labour and 'rent' of accommodation. Labour units are in the order of 1 man hour per 4–5 sq yd (around 4m^2). In broad terms direct costs will average 30% of gross income plus labour.

Pest and Disease Check

Aphis – use systemic sprays.
Carrot fly – use Disulfoton or Phorate.
Leaf miner – spray early with preventive chemical – Malathion D.D.T. etc.
Leaf spot – most seed is treated (Thiram) but spray with Benomyl or Captan.
Late blight (*cercospora*) – spray with Benomyl.
Root rots (*pythium*) – 'clean' propagation.
Soft rots – avoid excess nitrogen and high humidities and spray regularly with suitable fungicide.

Chinese Cabbage

Approx 2,500 seeds per 10 g.

Introduction

Although thought of as a 'new' vegetable, Chinese cabbage has been in cultivation for a considerable time, especially in Asia.

The increase in the Asian population of the U.K. has led to increased popularity in recent years.

There are more or less two basic species, pe-tsai (*Brassica pekinensis*) and pakchoi (*Brassica chinensis*).

Brassica pekinensis resembles cos lettuce with elongated but firm hearts or heads, whereas *Brassica chinensis* has a loose leaf habit, rather like Swiss Chard (spinach beet). Limited marketing experience in the U.K. shows greater demand for the heading type. Market demands must be carefully investigated – and areas with high Asian populations show biggest market potential.

Modern breeding has aimed at rapidly growing cultivars. Research into the cultural requirements of Chinese cabbage has been proceeding

116 Other Vegetables

at research centres including Lee Valley E.H.S., The Glasshouse Investigational Unit, Auchincruive (Ayrshire, Scotland) and elsewhere. In addition, plant raisers have also been researching methods of raising young plants for sale.

Cultural Requirements
Botanically speaking Chinese cabbage is an annual, with variable day length requirements according to breeding lines. Research shows the tendency to run to seed in short days but this varies much according to variety – with checks to growth possibly a more important factor than day length. The variety China King (F1) has given consistently good results at Auchincruive under cool glass. The crop likes an uninterrupted period of growth and seems more suitable for glasshouse or plastic structure culture in the U.K. – but it can be grown out of doors in summer with irrigation if necessary.

Seed Sowing
Germination of the seed is very rapid – within 24 hours at around 65°F (18°C). Seed is best sown thinly in *clean* compost with a pH of 6.5 and, like lettuce, a slightly higher level of nitrogen than the other main nutrients. *High salt contents must be avoided at both seedlings and cultural stage* – as this will predispose the plants to 'bolting' – especially if drying out coincides with high salts. As plants are ready very quickly for setting out, pricking off would not appear desirable – especially as it results in checks – and block- or strip-raising may be the best technique. Apart from the germination period high temperatures are not desirable.

Timetable
Research has aimed at resolving a year-round programme and this has in fact proved possible with unchecked growth, winter and summer, under cool frost-free protection with the right varieties. Poor light in the winter obviously slows up growth and delays the production programme. Note the need to pick 'short-term' varieties.

Planting
Soil should have a pH of 6.5, high nitrogen (index 1–2), medium phosphate and potash (index 2–3) with medium to low salt content. While soil should be clean sterilization is not required for successive crops for a limited period, but it may of course be necessary to sterilize where cultural programmes are extended. Spacing of plants is 11 × 11 in (28 × 28 cm) arranged in such a way to get maximum numbers into the structure or bed. Give frost-free conditions, ventilating freely above 70°F (21°C). Water regularly and *evenly*, avoiding drying out at edge of

Other Vegetables 117

beds as plants will show root death due to invasion of weak fungi and under dry high salt conditions.

Marketing
Cut and trim when 'heart' is fully formed and market in boxes according to market demand.

Economics
Broadly similar to lettuce (see page 103).

Pest and Disease Check
Slugs are very troublesome, especially in winter; root fly and caterpillars can be damaging also, and note that plant damage has been reported at Lee Valley under plastic with certain root fly preventive chemicals due to high temperatures.

Peach/potato aphid can be troublesome in summer. Earwigs and turnip flea beetle can be damaging – use H.C.H. dusts.

Chicory

Approx. 5,000–6,000 seeds per 10 g.

Introduction
This is a vegetable which is enjoying renewed popularity for its forced leaves or heads, otherwise known as chicons. It is however a very old salad vegetable indeed. The roots can be used as an additive to coffee. Botanically speaking it is *Cichorium intybus* – and probably a native of Europe or Asia. While markets are increasing, caution is desirable until an outlet is established.

Culture
Seed is sown in 'stale' clean seed beds – prepared in advance – which ideally have been cleaned up with Paraquat to deal with annual weeds. Sowing time is April or May but it is *inadvisable to sow too early* in case plants run to seed. Checks to growth should also be avoided – and ideally irrigation should be available to avoid drying out. Soil should be of pH 6–6.5 with reasonable levels of fertility but not freshly dressed with animal manure. Spacing is in drills ½ in (1.2 cm) deep, 15–18 in (38–45 cm) apart, and seeds should be space-sown by either hand (on small scale) or machine. Many of the small-scale hand seeders make an excellent job of sowing. The seedlings are thinned down to 8–9 in (20–23 cm) apart when large enough.

118 Other Vegetables

Whether to allow frosting or not before lifting roots has been the subject of some research (basically along the lines of rhubarb forcing) but it would not appear to make a great deal of difference. The tops of the plants are trimmed to 2 in (5 cm) and then the roots are lifted by hand or ploughed out of the ground in the autumn, hosed down to clean them and stored in a clean dry place, usually at the base of a building or wall, although vacant sheds could be used. Reasonably low temperatures at this stage would appear beneficial but straw should be used if temperatures get too low. It is advantageous if some grading of roots takes place as the size of head produced is usually in direct relationship to size of the root. Medium-sized roots are more acceptable. Some trimming of the roots at this stage may be required.

Forcing

There are various procedures which can be employed according to the facilities available.

If dark heated buildings are available to the 50°–60°F level (10°–15°C) – this is ideal. Other buildings can be used but darkness must be simulated by mats, or covering more deeply with soil, peat, sand or sawdust. The roots are taken out of the storage, their slender root tips removed, and stacked in suitable beds, closely together, with boards or other means to keep them upright if there is no soil in the ground. There should be some peat or fine soil worked between roots. If glasshouse or other borders are used a succession of trenches is dug and the roots are put in with their tops level with the soil. The roots are well watered and then covered lightly when in dark buildings or more deeply, up to 6–8 in (15–20 cm), in light buildings. While further watering may be required, do not soak covering material, a fear which should not arise if it is free draining. In three to four weeks at suitable temperatures chicons or heads should be formed, which are cut off at their base and marketed in trays. Ideal sizes are 3–4 in (7.5–10 cm) long, weighing 2–4 oz (50–100 g). The chicons may need some trimming. After harvesting the roots are removed and replaced with a further batch.

Economics

No accurate data available.

Troubles

Slugs are the main worry – use slug pellets. High temperatures at forcing should also be avoided by ventilation if weather is warm.

Varieties

The Belgian strain of Witloof is widely used although new varieties are coming forward.

Cress (and Mustard or Rape)

Cress – 350 seeds per g. Mustard/rape – 120/150 seeds per g.

Tends to be a specialized crop – grown for continuity. Cress seed is sown in summer, mustard/rape in winter (obtain salad types). It is a crop which needs good light and warmth, being ready for cutting in 10–14 days at around 60–65°F (15–18°C). While sterilized soils (or peat/sand composts spread on borders) were used, the crop these days tends to be grown in small punnets using capillary matting or other systems. After two days for germination artificial light may be used if need be at 8,000 lx on a continuous basis (24 hours) for three days. It is not a crop for the 'dabbler' and any grower would be advised to develop a market first – find out what is required, and then evolve a system back from there, on the basis of direct costs and labour.

Endive

A hardy type of lettuce. Sow June/July for covering with frames in autumn.

Gherkins

This is a crop very popular in Holland and Belgium as a 'follow on' from early strawberries, lettuce or other crops. They are 'mini cucumbers' and grown basically as cucumbers. Sow seed in early April in small pots, move on to larger pots, in JIP2 or soilless compost using 5 in (12.5 cm) pots. Apply liquid feed if required. Temperatures should be 60°F (15°C) night, 65°F (18°C), ventilating at 70°F (21°C). Plants are planted around May spaced as for cordon cucumbers (see page 81). They can also be grown on straw beds if necessary (see cucumbers) and trained as oblique cordons. Trim by removal of bottom two laterals and pruning side shoots to 5 leaves or allow to drop to 9–12 in (22.5–30 cm) above bed level before stopping. They are fed with high nitrogen feed – and treated basically as shorter term cucumbers.

Harvesting
Pick over regularly up to 5 days per week, and market in trays.

Economics
Check that crop will be received in markets or seek contract with canner. High yields are possible up to 40 ton/acre (100 tonne/ha) *cold grown* which shows the potential with heat. Note the danger of imports from

Other Vegetables

warm countries. Input costs are not high. See cucumbers for more detail.

Herbs and Other Crops

There is limited demand for protected crops of herbs, especially in winter. This includes items such as parsley (see page 125), fennel, sage, thyme, which are ideal crops for plastic structures. There may also be scope for crops such as kohlrabi (see below) and spinach beet – for production earlier or later than mainstream production. Interesting work is proceeding at Lee Valley E.H.S. (Hertfordshire) in this direction (see kohlrabi). Grow herbs generally from box-sown seed germinated in spring – early summer and planted at 12 × 12 in (30 × 30 cm).

Kohlrabi

This cross between turnip and cabbage is a crop which grows in poor dry soils.

It is being well received in markets, and would appear to offer scope for protected cropping.

Sown direct in drills from March, 12–18 in (30–45 cm) apart, it is thinned to a stand.

Leeks

Approx. 3,000–4,000 seeds per 10 g. 250 g/acre (650 g/ha) for transplanting. For direct drilling use graded natural seed approx. 1 kg per acre (2½ kg/ha) or pelleted seed to count (plant population 60,000 – 90,000 acre: 200,000 – 220,000 ha).

Traditionally an outdoor crop – leeks are sown under protection in glasshouses, plastics or frames, cold or with mild heat in January or February, in boxes, seed beds or multi-blocks (3 plants per 4.3 cm blocks for early crop – up to 6–7 plants per 7.5 cm blocks for later crops).

Planting out takes place as soon as practical for the early crop at spacings of 4–6 in (10–15 cm). (Alternatively the seed is drilled direct.)

Soils must be well supplied with organic matter, pH around 6 with N.P.K. indices 1.3.4. Weed control is important.

The transition to protected cropping allows for much earlier and denser planting – row widths of 10–12 ins (25–30 cm). The same applies to direct sowing systems.

Other Vegetables

Experience is needed with this crop under protection, especially for early marketing, owing to a combination of day length and temperature.

Irrigation is especially important for the protected crop. Market the crop in bundles.

Economics

	sq yd	m²
Target yield	6–8 lbs	3–4 kg
Plants sq yd	28–20 plants	20–22
Seed	.2 g (approx.)	.25 g (approx.)
Fertilizers	2–5 oz	56–140 g

Packaging according to demand. Marketing = 12–14% of gross income.

Labour Units

1 man hour 4–6 sq yd/5.5m²

Pest and Disease Check

Onion fly – use treated seed and treat blocks with Gamma H.C.H.

Marrows and Courgettes

This is a crop undergoing changes in culture – and is of interest under plastics as a crop offering better return than lettuce. Basically speaking under the protection of plastics *courgettes* are grown and outdoors the larger marrows are allowed to mature. Seed is sown direct in peat pots or soil/peat blocks (or bought in as blocks) for planting in frost-free protection. Spacing is around 20 × 20 in (50 × 50 cm) or wider apart: in good soil pH 6 with balanced fertilizer 10–10–10. While plants may be allowed to sprawl, some training on strings or nets is now favoured. Pollination takes place with bees or other insects. A late autumn crop may also be grown, sowing seed in July and planting in August.

Economics

Yields vary greatly according to training methods but high yields are possible with training systems; 14–16 sq yd (15–22 m²) are average (average weight 1.50 kg/m²). Control aphids and look out for *botrytis*.

Melons

It is not thought that this is an economic proposition in temperate Europe – except as a 'fill in' crop where vacant space under protection

122 Other Vegetables

allows. There can be no more delicious fruit than the melon, and a few grown on the bench following propagation activities can be both interesting and rewarding. It must be borne in mind, however, that imported melons can be bought very cheaply and it is pointless to waste considerable time and money on fuel to grow them in temperate zones.

Preparation
Production programme is as follows:

Seed sown	Planted	Harvested
In greenhouse March/April	April/early May	July/August
In cold frames Seed sown in greenhouse March/April	April/May	August/September

It was invariably at one time the practice to make up 'hot beds' with fresh manure in continuous ridges some 12–18 in (30–45 cm) high with some clean soil on top of the ridge. This raises problems, however, with the ammonia gas given off by the manure in greenhouses. More usually these days a mixture of good riddled loam with $1/5$ or $1/6$ part of well-rotted farmyard manure or leaf mould to give the necessary 'body' to the compost is used or alternatively compost to John Innes No. 2 Compost standard. In the interests of economy, mounds instead of continuous ridges are more practical, especially for the shorter term crop. Some means of support on wires or a trellis must be provided. Nutritional standards are a pH of 6; soil indices N:P:K 2-3-4.

Sowing and Planting
Seed is sown as for cucumber, singly in pots, in John Innes No. 1 or soilless equivalent, germinating at a temperature of 65–70°F (18–21°C).

Good hygiene is essential as the seedlings are very disease-prone. While potting on can be practised as for cucumbers, it is more usual to leave seedlings in their germinating pots or blocks, feeding with diluted liquid feed if necessary to sustain growth. The plants are given all the light available. If plants need support, provide this with a cane.

Plant carefully at 2½ ft/67 cm spacing when the compost is around 65–68°F (18–20°C) leaving the root ball proud of the soil or compost. Water in well, ensuring that there are no air pockets below the root ball. A frequent mistake is to break the root ball and the resulting check on planting can have serious long-term effects by allowing the entry of disease.

Other Vegetables 123

Cultivation
Training by strings or wires is of first importance. The leading shoot is taken to the top of the support before removing the growing tip to encourage side shoots which bear the flowers. Melons have separate male and female flowers. Pollination of the female flowers by removing the flat male flower and inserting this into the centre of the open female flower is necessary, or allow free entry of insects when the sun is shining. The shoots are tied into the support. Individual support for the melons by use of small nets is desirable at a later stage. Try to maintain a warm atmosphere around 60–65°F (16–18°C) or higher as far as this is practical if a mixed growing house is involved and water regularly to avoid drying out, keeping water away from the main stem; it helps to protect this with a few pieces of broken pot, but avoid saturation of the compost.

Top dress with a good loam or peat (plus a little lime to offset its acidity) when white roots are seen on the surface. A good balanced liquid fertilizer should also be applied regularly, Organic based Maxicrop Tomato Special is ideal for producing superlative quality fruits and avoiding chemical damage. Allowing plants to sprawl is the more usual technique in warmer areas, spacing plants 2–3 ft (60–90 cm) apart. This is the method employed in Spain, Southern France and Italy for protected crops. It can also be done in the UK.

Economics
This crop is little grown in temperate zones, but the growing costs are broadly similar to courgettes or marrows, with higher returns for fruits (see page 121).

Pest and Disease Check
Botrytis, *fusarium*, neck root and whitefly. Observe good hygiene and spray regularly with insecticide.

Mushrooms

Mushrooms can be a worthwhile crop if properly grown. Ideally there should be a cellar, well-insulated shed or black insulated double-skinned polythene structure available. They are a very tricky crop, demanding attention to every detail, and 'dabblers' should seek expert help. They involve much manual handling as a crop when grown on a small scale and mechanical equipment is not available; this tends to make them less attractive than appears at first sight. A number of firms sell spawn and other material and give cultural directions for mushroom growing.

124 Other Vegetables

Help is also given with marketing if a sufficient supply is available. The 'calamity' rate can be very high, however, and successions of enthusiasts start off well but fall by the wayside.

Preparation

A readily available and continuous supply of horse manure straw or other organic matter to make the growing compost is essential. If mushrooms are to be grown on a continuous basis, some form of heating for the building or structure concerned will also be required. If summer cropping only, no artificial heat is necessary. Buildings must be scrupulously clean and properly ventilated to avoid excess humidity. Darkness is preferable but not vital. Mushrooms can be grown in beds on the ground, but 3 × 2 ft (90 × 60 cm) stacking trays or tiered slatted benches make best use of available space in buildings.

Allow a period of 6–8 weeks after spawning before cropping begins, which should then extend for 3–4 months.

Straw horse manure or other organic matter is stacked in square heaps of about 1.5 × 1.5 m (5 × 5 ft) not more than 1.5 m/5 ft high. These are soaked thoroughly, using a mild antiseptic such as 4 ml Lysol per 5 litres water (1 teaspoon per gallon). Turn the outside to the inside after 7–8 days and add more water if necessary. Repeat this every five days or so (when the heap has heated) until uniform in temperature and moisture. Turning a total of 4–5 times is generally required. Alternatively straw and special compost-makers can be used, following instructions supplied with the compost-maker. Beds are then made up from the compost, 1.2 m wide and 9–10 in (22–25 cm) deep in summer, 12–15 in (30–38 cm) in winter, or 8 in (20 cm) deep in trays. Beds can also be made up out of doors in a ridge from a base 76 cm/30 in wide, tapering to 5 in (12 cm) at a height of 24 in (60 cm).

Spawning

Allow ventilation of the building or structure for a few days after making up beds or filling trays. When compost temperature drops to 70–75°F (21–24°C) insert spawn or 'grain' bought from a specialist supplier every 10 in/25 cm or according to directions given.

Cultivation

In 7–9 days when the mycelium or 'roots' can be seen developing from the spawn, cover with a 1–2 in (2.5–5 cm) layer of peat with ground limestone added at approximately 1½ lb per bushel (1–1.2 kg per 50 litres) to render it alkaline. Beds are kept dry at first, then well watered. Mushrooms will develop according to temperature levels.

Other Vegetables

Economics
Yield 25–27lb/yd/13–14kg/m²
Direct costs 30–40% of gross income.
Labour units 1 sq yd per man hour (.09 m²/approx.), or higher according to scale of operation.

Pest and Disease Check
Strict attention must be given to management and any pest attack dealt with immediately. Diseases, when they occur, can be disastrous, as conditions for their development are ideal, and they can quickly wipe out the whole crop. Enthusiasts are urged to obtain full details on pests and diseases from suppliers of spawn, there being a wealth of detailed and accurate information available – including economics which can be over-optimistic.

Onions (and Leeks) in Blocks

Specialist firms are producing onions and leeks in peat blocks for planting outdoors, either multi- or single-seeded. This is a 'crop' likely to escalate and could be lucrative (3–7 plants per block).

Spring or Salad Onions

This is a crop which is being grown on an increasing scale with production for the early spring and 'late' crop. It can be sown in January/February (according to region) in cool glass or plastic structure in drills 6–8 in (15–18 cm) apart at seed rate approx. 3–4 g per sq yd/m². Soil should be cleaned by sterilization or chemical weedkillers used. The crop is marketed in bunches. Direct costs of production average 30% of gross return.

Parsley

Approx. 5,000 seeds per 10 g.

A crop which shows excellent potential for cool glass or plastic structures to give better continuity of cropping during winter periods.

Sow seed in July, thinly in boxes or borders – to plant under cover at around 12 × 12 in (30 × 30 cm) in August/September. Soil should be reasonably well supplied with N.P.K. Supply plenty of water and ventilate well.

Yield very variable according to conditions – but a good money

Other Vegetables

spinner. Aim to pull 3 lb/sq yd (1½ kg/m²). Labour units low – 1 man hour per 10–12 sq yd (11 m).

Radish

This is a crop which is becoming important – and variety breeding work by seed companies such as Rijk – Zwaan (Netherlands) is helping to make radishes a year-round possibility.

Levels of natural light are critical in winter – and in many areas may render out-of-season production completely impossible or certainly not economically feasible. Space sowing of radish to grow under artificial light (15,000 lx 24 hours) for 21 days after a two-day germination period is a technique which has developed to some extent, but scale of growing in relation to capital investment is critical. Light soils are a great asset to production both in winter and generally. Radish is highly salt sensitive – so fertilizer levels should be low. In fertile soils no base dressing is generally required – but this should be checked by analysis. Nitrogen levels should be low, Index 1, Phosphate and Potash Index 3–4. Base feeds if required should be high: Potash 10–10–20 in summer – 10–10–15 in winter – at rates indicated by analysis; pH should be 6–6.5 For successive crops analysis is important.

Seed Sowing

This on any scale is best done by precision sowers. Row spacings for Venlo Structures (3.2 m) range from 30 to 42 rows per bay.

More seeds are needed in winter than summer, the range being from 2 g/m² (March/August) up to 4.5 g/m² in winter. Experience is needed to determine optimum seeding rates. For artificial lighting seed is space or thinly sown in boxes, and this technique is also extending to greenhouse culture.

Temperatures and Humidity

For greenhouse structures aim to sow when temperatures are not lower than 41°F (5°C) at night with a day temperature 50°F (10°C). *But note that light levels are critical. Frost protection is essential.* Excess humidity is not desirable and temperature *boosting* is favoured. To do this let the temperature rise for one hour as high as possible with heating system in operation, then open vents to let moisture-laden air expel and shut vents again. CO_2 enrichment is useful in warm weather.

Watering

Radishes do not relish excess watering. Ensure uniform moisture for

Other Vegetables 127

germination and then 'play it by ear'. When leaves show dark coloration or limpness this is indicative of water requirement.

Harvesting
Rijk-Zwaan list intended sowing to harvesting periods – which varies from 9–12 weeks with plant densities from 100 to 300 per sq yd (120–380 m²). This is around 8–24 (10–12 radishes) bundles sq yd (10–28 m²). The through-put varies but at best 5–6 crops can be produced per year *if* there is no disease problem – which shows the high potential of the crop. Cost of seed fertilizer and heat on a pro rata basis is not difficult to calculate but on average direct costs (less labour) are likely to be 20–25% of gross return. The crop is marketed in trays containing 10–12 bunches.

Labour input will also vary according to equipment available and timing of crop (for watering etc.) but it would seem that one man hour per 5–6 sq yd (4–5 m²) per crop is average.

Pest and Disease Check
Pithiness – inside of root goes spongy and/or shows holes. Avoid growing irregularities, especially water. Varies with variety.
Splitting – caused by spurts of growth in spring. Again varies with variety.
Coarse tails – lateral roots develop spoiling shape. Avoid watering too near harvesting.
Mildew – avoid excess humidity. Spray or dust with Zineb. More space advisable for crop in future.
Root rots – caused by *Rhizocotonia sclerotinia* and *alternaria*. Plants wilt and die off in patches. Several different fungi could be involved with secondary infection with *botrytis*. Use Quintozene dust pre-sowing or pre-emergence. Sterilize soil for future crops especially for *alternaria*.
Slugs, Woodlice – plants eaten. Use baits.
Leatherjackets – use baits regularly and sterilize for future.

Rhubarb (Forced)

Introduction
High fuel and labour costs coupled with imports have had the result of drastically reducing areas of forced rhubarb grown in the U.K.: 1,012 acres (404 ha) in 1966 to 422 acres (168 ha) in 1980.

Market outlets must be carefully investigated before becoming deeply involved as it is an expensive crop to develop in terms of stock and suitable insulated buildings – although in the latter context double-

128 Other Vegetables

skinned insulated black polythene structures can be used. Suitable buildings can of course serve rhubarb forcing in winter, and mushrooms in summer/autumn, or for that matter switch between the two crops on a total involvement basis. Most research in the U.K. is centred at Stockbridge House E.H.S., Selby, Yorkshire. Work under investigation there includes:

1 Extension of forcing season – using dormancy preventing growth regulators – or selection of suitable strains requiring very short days to induce dormancy.
2 Development of labour-saving methods – including growing in containers.
3 Utilization of cheaper forcing sheds i.e. insulated multi-bay plastics – double-tiered facilities.
4 Market research.
5 Selection and promotion of new varieties for specific purposes.
6 Refined propagation techniques.

Propagation
While rhubarb can be grown from seed, this method is both long term and uncertain due to the variability of seed production. Vegetative propagation by division (as 'sets') is the normal method, and it would be necessary to obtain stock as free as possible from virus diseases, although tissue culture is developing for many crops including rhubarb.

Valuable work has been undertaken at Stockbridge House E.H.S., and elsewhere on 'cleaning up' stock. Trials have shown the value of virus-free stock for increased yields on both 'field' and forcing crops.

Divided crowns or sets (note development of rapid propagation in pots) are established in fertile clean land, pH.7, N index 1, P.K. indices 3–4 at suitable spacings for mechanical equipment – usually 2½ × 3 ft (75 × 90 cm) which is 5,808 crowns per acre (approx. 14,395/ha).

Residual weedkillers such as Simazine at 3 lb A.1 per acre (3.3 kg/ha) are applied annually (variable rates). To encourage field growth nitrogen should be applied on several occasions, 4 cwt per acre (500 kg/ha) post-planting, up to 10 cwt per acre (1,255 kg/ha) in the spring prior to forcing.

Preparation for Forcing
Crowns for forcing must be at least 2 years old (preferably 3). They are in early autumn ploughed out of the ground and left on the surface to be frosted.

In the meantime 'conventional' methods are followed, checking the cold units prior to lifting. This is done by using an angled soil thermometer, carefully inserted with the graduated tube level with the ground surface – check daily at 9.00 a.m. G.M.T. (10.00 a.m. before

Other Vegetables

Summer Time ends). All readings below 49°F (9°C) are added up on a cold unit system – to determine the optimum degree of 'cold treatment' – to hasten and improve production under forcing conditions.

This can vary from around 200 units F (where 1 unit = 1°F) for the variety Timperley Early to 520 units for Victoria (111–280 units – Celsius). 'Cold units' applicable is however a variable issue – according to stock quality.

Forcing

The crowns are generally ploughed out with as little damage as possible and transported by as economical labour use as practical (bogey rails are used on some large farms) to the forcing sheds, where they are packed into beds 5–6 ft (1.5–1.8 m) wide (number will vary per sq yd/m^2). Clean soil or peat is used to pack spaces between crowns.

Complete darkness, moisture and warmth will induce blanched shoots to form. Ideal forcing temperatures are around 55°F (13°C) with adequate ventilation to avoid 'soft head' and *botrytis*.

Successive batches can be forced to give continuity. Pick with candles or torches for light.

Economics

In broad terms aim to pull 40 lb/sq yd (21 kg/m^2) and market in polythene sleeved bundles in 14 lb cardboard boxes. The rhubarb crop is very difficult to cost out. The following summary from Stockbridge House E.H.S. gives useful guidance.

Costs per box up to point of sale (London Market) 1979

Yield per Root lb	Yield per* 6000 Roots Ton	Number Boxes	Growing Cost pence	Marketing Cost pence	Total Cost per box	Cost Per lb pence
4	10.7	1714	76	90	166	11.9
5	13.4	2142	60	90	150	10.7
6	16.1	2574	50	90	140	10.0
7	18.7	3000	43	90	133	9.5
8	21.4	3428	38	90	128	9.1

*600 yards of shed; one acre outdoor land

In order to calculate the profit margin subtract the cost per box from the net return box (i.e. gross return less 10% commission). *Fixed costs are not included.*

There is research proceeding on whether or not coldness is required prior to forcing – or dormancy is 'short day' induced – and it is possible that dormancy can be chemically induced.

Other Vegetables

Sweet Peppers

Approx. 150 seeds per g.

Introduction
Peppers belong to the genus *capsicum* – but are very different from the commercial pepper which is another species. They are probably natives of tropical America, although numerous so-called species have been attributed to southern Asia. Modern varieties of sweet peppers are hybrids selected for fruit size and shape, habit of growth, seasonality and resistance to certain diseases, especially virus. Continental travel has done much to popularize peppers for the salad bowl but marketing surveys are essential if growing on any scale is contemplated.

Timetable
The pepper has very similar requirements to the tomato although light levels are not so critical. Note also the lower air temperatures at which peppers should be grown to induce setting of fruits.

Approximate Programmes (which may vary considerably according to circumstances)

	Sow	Plant	'Season' time
Very Early Heated Crop	Mid-end Nov.	End Nov/Dec	60–75 days
Early Heated Crop	Mid-end Jan.	End Jan/mid Feb.	70–80 days
'Heated' Crop (for protection)	Mid-end Mar.	End Mar/April	55–65 days
Cold Crop	Mid April/early May	Late April/mid May	45–55 days
Autumn Crop (heat may be required)	Mid June/early July	End June/20th July	40–45 days

Research is proceeding into long-term culture of peppers.

Seed Sowing
Sow seed in open compost at high temperatures of around 75° – 82°F (24° – 28°C) as this gives speedy uniform germination.

Pricking Off
Prick off into soil/peat blocks or peat pots around 8–10 cm in size (the larger size for delayed planting which may be desirable for the early

Other Vegetables 131

heated crop). Where it is intended to crop the plants in pots of plastic or whale hides, prick off into smaller blocks, 5–6 cm, or smaller peat pots.

Compost should be of pH 5.8–6.3 with medium levels of N.P.K. *High salts must be avoided* (see tomatoes, page 64).

Give plants good light and space out as required holding temperatures at not less than 72°–75°F (22°–24°C) if this is practical and maximum growth rate is desired. Lower temperatures will suffice but planting can be delayed. Time of propagation can vary from 4–6 weeks under best conditions to 8–10 weeks or longer. Note the remarks which come later about fruit setting at lower temperatures.

Planting and Spacing
This can be at 18 in (45 cm) square where 4 shoots are left with no plant pruning or down to 16 in (40 cm) where 2 shoots are taken and plants trimmed by lateral stopping to 1–3 leaves. There is much to favour the wider planting system if labour costs are to be kept low. Plants are set out before they are 'crowding' and ideally when they are in flower. It is important to avoid root severance by standing the plants on a thin layer of peat or other method. Border soil temperatures should be high, 72°–75°F (22°–24°C) for maximum growth, this ideally by soil warming, but again compromise is necessary to keep the crop economically viable. (Research is proceeding on peppers under N.F.T. and rock wool systems.)

Soil Conditions
Border soils should be adjusted to a pH of 5.8–6.3 with N.P.K. magnesium index around 1.3.4 with medium salt content only. Soil sterilization by heat or by chemicals is required for successive crops to avoid the root troubles typical of the tomato crop. The pepper is a crop which although responding to good aerial day temperatures sets better at lower temperatures. General recommendations for good setting are 59–63°F (15–17°C) night and around 65–68°F (18–20°C) day – ventilating above 73–75°F (23°C) in sunny weather, but in dull weather temperatures are lower both night and day. *Note that this applies also to propagation stage where planting is delayed and plants are actually in flower.* Pepper is a crop which appears to respond to high soil temperatures and lower air temperatures which makes it ideal for soil warming by electricity or water pipes and especially for N.F.T.

Support stems are taken on a 2- or 4-stem basis according to system practised. If the 4-stem system is followed horizontal strings will be necessary to contain the plants.

The length of the growing season is extending as new varieties are introduced and cultural information accrued, but broadly speaking at

132 Other Vegetables

this stage it appears best to have successive crops rather than take a long-season crop due to the environmental problems which can develop in cluttered growing conditions.

Economics
See aubergines, but yields and labour units higher.

Troubles
Basically similar to tomatoes, although *begonia* mite appears to affect peppers. Fruit blotch due to high salts is likely, especially if environmental conditions vary excessively. Virus has been shown to be a serious problem. Aphis is a constant plague.

Sweet Corn

Seed count 44–66 g.

A crop which has been grown with some success in cold glass or plastic structures. Seed is best sown in April/early May in plastic pots or blocks for planting at approximately 18 in (45 cm) × 15 in (38 cm) three weeks in advance of outdoor planting time in well-prepared soil. Research shows that soil or peat blocks should be large enough to avoid planting checks. Can also be sown direct, thinning seed out to required spacing, but this can mean a later crop. Liquid feed is given if required. Help with pollination is necessary from male flowers to fertilize female flower by tapping or spraying.

Yield is approximtely 2½ cobs per plant. It is a very low-cost crop however, and may be more lucrative than lettuce. It is relatively pest- and disease-free.

Can be well received in local markets, but this is a crop which is widely grown in warm climates and is imported in quantity.
Labour units are 1 man hour per 12-14 sq yd (13 m^2).

Seakale (Crambe maritima)

A batch of plants is raised initially by sowing seed out of doors in April in deeply dug soil enriched with manure. Seed is sown thinly in drills 12in (30 cm) apart, ¾ in (2 cm) deep. Seedlings are thinned to 6 in (15 cm) apart. Plants are kept well hoed and free from weeds and left undisturbed until the following February or March, when they are lifted and planted about 2½ ft (75 cm) apart each way in a well-prepared site. Prevent a flowering stem from forming by cutting off the crown of each plant *when planting*, just below soil level. In autumn trim off and save for root cuttings all but the central root (it is important to make a straight cut at the top and a slanting cut at the base of the cuttings). Pack the roots closely together under greenhouse staging or in boxes of good soil. If given a temperature of 45–50°F (7–10°C), plenty of water and complete darkness, succulent blanched shoots will be produced which are ready for use when 6 in (15 cm) long. Once the roots have been forced they are destroyed, after removing any suitably sized sections to reserve as a further source of cuttings.

The side shoots or root cuttings are stored in batches for planting outdoors the following February or March. They are set out vertically in well-prepared soil in dibber holes 16–18 in (40–45 cm) apart in rows 2 ft (50 cm) apart with the top (straight cut) of the cutting just below the soil surface. Limit the plant to one strong shoot. These plants will provide a further supply of forcing roots in the autumn.

Economics

No meaningful data available.

Turnip

4,000 seeds per 10 g.

A crop with some potential for early crops under either heated or cold glass or plastic. It has doubtful economic value for the late crop due to clashes with hardy outdoor types. It may also be grown in frames or other forms of shelter.

Soils should ideally be friable and organic, pH 6–5–7. Medium levels of N.P.K.

Sow Purple Top or white types first – followed by Golden. With heat around 55–60°F (13–15°C) can be sown in January (good light areas only) in drills 12 in (30 cm) apart.

1 g seed per 3–4 sq yd (3.5 m^2) or broadcast on well-firmed beds at approximately 1 g seed per sq yd/m^2.

Adequate moisture is essential plus good ventilation to avoid stress, otherwise running to seed or leaf is likely – especially in poor light areas.

Market in bunches of 4–6 aiming for 6–8 bunches per sq yd (around 7 per m^2).

Labour units are 1 man hour per 6–7 sq yd (5 m^2).

Pests to check for are flea beetle and slugs – diseases are mildew and *botrytis*.

Chapter Fifteen

Nutrient Film Techniques (N.F.T.) And Rock Wool Systems

Hydroponics in its various forms is not a new technique and is primarily concerned with the growing of plants in nutrient solutions instead of conventionally in soil. It is being used for a wide range of crops.

The word 'hydroponics' is derived from two Greek words 'hydro' (water) and 'ponus' (labour) and was conceived by Dr. W. F. Gericke of California, U.S.A., who is given credit for first carrying out hydroponics on a commercial scale in the early 1930s. Dr. Gericke was following on from a wide miscellany of research work dating back to 1699, when somewhat unwittingly a scientist called John Woodward started the whole science of soilless plant cultivation, deriving the nutrients ironically enough by adding soil to water!

Readers wishing further historical and technical data are referred to the book *Hydroponics* by Dudley Harris (U.K. edition revised by A. M. M. Berrie and I. G. Walls).

Basic Concepts

All plants rely on nutrient solutions for their growth – and soil could be called a complete substrate consisting of (1) organic and (b) inorganic fractions.
(a) is sub-divided into living and non-living content, the former consisting of bacteria, fungi, protozoa, worms and small animals. The combined effect of the living organic content is to convert the non-living organic material, consisting of plant and animal remains, bulky organic materials applied to soil – such as farmyard manure, peat, organic

fertilizers etc. into basic constituent form – or simple chemical elements which can be used by plants for their vital growth processes when dissolved in soil water.
(b) The inorganic fraction of the soil consists of chemically broken down rock particles which also complement the nutrient content of soil water.

Both the organic and inorganic (chemical) activity of soils is a continual process, influenced by many factors, principally temperature and air/water content, so it follows that plant growth is variable. Coupled with this is the possible build up of pests and diseases and the difficulty and costs of controlling them.

Hydroponics in its various forms aims to by-pass organic and inorganic activity, and supply the plants with a man-controlled supply of nutrients using 'sterile' facilities at the beginning of each crop phase.

Development Stages of Hydroponics

It is difficult to say with any certainty which came first of the two stages, (a) use of inert aggregates or (b) growing plants with roots suspended in aerated nutrient solutions with no aggregate.

One thing which has clearly emerged over the years is that in the case of (a) considerable quantities of inert (or nearly so) aggregate is required – and as these initially were gravels or sand, their purchase and transport involves considerable cost. As for (b) this concerned a considerable amount of fairly sophisticated and costly equipment.

Relating the drawbacks of these initial systems to modern costs created extreme economic difficulties. It was in consequence of this that researchers around the world have over the years and indeed are still seeking ways and means of reducing initial and running costs on hydroponic systems and simultaneously linking these to the high crop yields necessary under intensive cropping conditions especially under protection with the high investment and running costs involved in today's inflationary scene (see aeroponics, page 149). Things have gone two ways:
(a) The aggregate scene has changed considerably and in place of bulky and heavy aggregates, materials such as 'rock wool' (see page 145) and other 'inert' media (or substrates) such as perlite and vermiculite have made their appearance. Some of these systems would seem to be economically acceptable and have very high yield potential. Peat and wood bark systems, while strictly speaking not hydroponics because of their organic nature, and behaviour as 'soil' in many ways, cannot be completely divorced from aggregate systems. *It seems very likely that there will be still further development into aggregate systems, provided they involve low cost substrates.*
(b) Within the concept of nutrient solution systems there have been many developments and it was from a miscellany of these that the

system, developed at the Glasshouse Crops Research Institute, Littlehampton, Sussex, England (G.C.R.I.) by Dr. Alan Cooper, and other researchers, has in the late 1970s swept the world as an economically practical system with high yield potential.

Crops are grown in a shallow film of re-circulating nutrient solution with or without capillary matting in troughs made of various materials. Capital costs are relatively low and results are readily repeatable. Such systems have been given the 'label' N.F.T. (Nutrient Film Technique).

There has in addition been the related systems of crop production for items such as lettuce and pot plants using re-circulating nutrient solutions with or without substrates and with or without capillary matting. The present trend with crops such as lettuce etc. is to produce these on hydroponic systems actually growing to 'point of sale'. N.F.T. systems are of particular significance in hot arid countries where soil is unsuitable or non-existent and water supplies limited. It is no accident therefore that N.F.T. production units are being set up in these countries where crop growth was at one time thought impossible. This development is by no means unique to modern times and it should be noted that massive food production units were set up during World War II in the Pacific for U.S. Forces, primarily on a nutrient tank basis and Dudley Harris ('Hydroponics') also refers to large installations in sand and gravel at Oranjemund, South West Africa, which have been established and functioning for many years.

N.F.T. – Its Present Stage of Development and Practical Stages in Setting Up

The layout and design of N.F.T. systems can follow many varied patterns. For tomatoes, cucumbers and other 'tall' crops, plastic sloping gullies, laid on sloping ground, sloping boards, elevated sloping metal stands, polystyrene slabs or flat surfaces generally, carry a film of constantly re-circulating nutrient solution.

Recent years have seen much change in physical design from rigid pre-formed plastic gullies to cheaper thin film plastic gullies using thin gauge black/white polythene with or without a base layer of capillary matting. It is usual to design these gullies with a slope of not less than 1–100 and more recently with a 'platform' in the middle so that plants can stay proud of the nutrient. The basic object is to have an even film of nutrient not greater than ¼ in (6–7 mm). The gulley width lies between 9 and 12 in (22.5–30 cm). Adjustable stands may be used to create a suitable slope to keep the nutrient moving quickly. The basic layout and design of a nutrient system is shown in Figure 7. Systems can be any size but obviously must be tailored to the size of unit available. The U.K. chemical company I.C.I. state that the nutrient sump should be of a capacity of 500 gallons per acre (5,500 litres/ha)

138 Nutrient Film Techniques and Rock Wool Systems

for a protected area in temperate zones. Due to transpiration loss and evaporation losses probably greater reserve is needed in tropical climates. The nutrient tank scale laid down by the firm Nutriculture Ltd., of Sandy Lane, Ormskirk, Lancashire, is 1 gallon per 5 tomatoes (1 litre to 1 tomato) or for lettuce systems 1 gallon per 25 lettuce (1 litre to 5 lettuce). Flow rates for the nutrient can vary but is in the general order of 20 gallons per 100 ft of trough (90 litres/30 m) but the flow can be higher or lower according to circumstances. One can purchase N.F.T. 'kits' for smaller unit production.

Firms providing N.F.T. equipment will quote pump sizes necessary for different scales of units and also supply all the fitments although it is feasible to install systems on a 'do-it-yourself' basis and probably cheaper too. Referring to Figure 7 the main elements are lettered as follows:–

A. Supply tank on the basis of 500 gallons per acre (5,500 litres/ha).
B. Pump of adequate size for size of unit, submersible or an outside type.

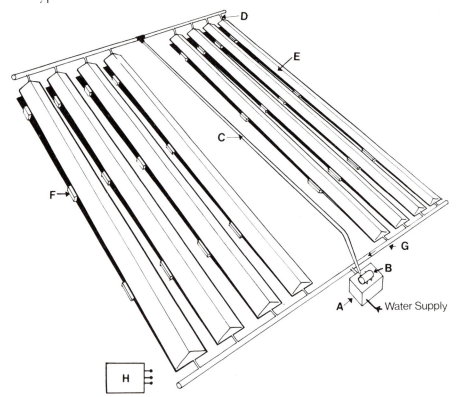

Figure 7 Nutrient Film Technique typical lay-out. (By kind permission of Nutriculture Ltd., Sandy Lane, Ormskirk.)

C. Supply pipe or pipes to troughs usually ½ in –2 in (1.25 – 5 cm) made of polythene or alkathene.
D. Feed tubes invariably of 6 mm diameter.
E. Troughs rigid or made up with polystyrene centre platform or made up with black/white polythene (white outside) 12–24 in wide (30–60 cm).
F. Metal tray on stands or soil adjusted to give sufficient slope which should be not less than 1–100.
G. Gulley flowing back to supply tank noting that filters will be required, size of fittings related to number of outlets.
H. According to levels of sophistication nutrient supply concentrate tank along with nutrient monitoring control gear as specified by design. Facilities for heating nutrient solution are invariably necessary in temperate zones with a submersible electric heater or other method to maintain around 77°F (25°C).

N.F.T. for Lettuce or Low Crops Including Pot Plants

Basically speaking the same equipment is required with black/white polythene overlaid on sloping concrete flattened soil or alternatively multiduct channels used with or without capillary matting on continuous or intermittent flow. Lettuce, fruits (strawberries) or pot plant culture is going through a considerable development phase in the 1980s and it is impossible at this stage to lay down precise specifications, including the decision whether 'underground' heating is required or not. Strict costing is necessary to decide whether the costs of setting up N.F.T. lettuce systems are justified in a normal cropping situation where good soil is available, things being different in a 'no soil' area, especially in an arid climate.

It must be borne in mind that the quality of lettuce is also very high on conventional cultural systems and there would require to be a definite reason for venturing into N.F.T., the main move in the early 1980s being towards the marketing of 'growing' crops.

Costings for N.F.T.

It is a fairly simple matter to cost out the setting up of an N.F.T. system in any particular situation and allied to this must be the running costs, including nutrients through the season (see Chapter 5).

Basic Considerations for All N.F.T. Systems

Having set up the physical method of supplying the crops with nutrients on continuous or intermittent flow, costed the project in relation to problems of using disease- or pest-infested soils or no soils at all, potential crop yields (I.C.I. quote tomato yields *well* in excess of 100 tons/acre/250 tonnes/ha: this is borne out by many leading growers in Guernsey and elsewhere), the next stage is to learn the techniques involved in N.F.T.

This is something where a little experience and expert help goes a very long way (note in this context there are consultants and firms able to set up and monitor projects on a 'packaged' basis).

There is a very definite trend, especially in Holland, in the early 1980s to move in to 'horizontal' forms of N.F.T., avoiding the high water usage of flow systems presently much in vogue in the U.K. and throughout the world. This invariably involves some form of substrate such as rock wool (see page 145). What in effect is happening is a marriage between N.F.T. and substrate systems, returning in many ways to the original concepts of hydroponics.

Nutrient Control

Obviously the most critical aspect of N.F.T. is nutrient control, and supplying the plants with the correct balance of nutrients relative to the water supply of the area and maintaining this situation in face of crop uptake of nutrients, evaporation loss, etc.

On a *very* small scale nutrient replacement every few weeks can be effective and avoids complications. First and foremost should be an analysis of water supply not only for pH but for the presence or absence of various elements. These include magnesium, calcium, iron, manganese, molybdenum, copper, chlorine and zinc. Where this analysis shows large quantities of trace elements to be present in the water supply, they could quickly build up to toxic levels demanding modification of a 'starter' solution which can invariably mean going on to self-formulated or specially prescribed feeds. Several courses of action now follow.

1 Decide to manually control monitoring of nutrients on the basis of pH (by liquid indicator or pH meter) and conductivity levels in mhos (microsiemens) (2,000–2,500 cucumbers, 2,500–3,000 tomatoes) (using a conductivity meter).
2 Install 'automatic' controllers which monitor and adjust pH and nutrient levels.
3 Purchase proprietary feeds and follow the full directions given with these.

It is not within the scope or practicality of this book to give all details of the different feeds and various equipment on their practical management other than present the broad parameters or procedures.

I.C.I. give the following directions using their Solufeed F which was introduced in 1975. This information is taken from the Solufeed leaflet dated November 1978.

Nutrient Film Techniques and Rock Wool Systems

Preparation of Nutrient Solutions

1 'Solufeed' F
The stock solution is prepared by dissolving 25 kg of 'Solufeed' F in 170 litres (38 gals) of water.

2 Calcium Nitrate
The stock solution is prepared by dissolving 15 kg of calcium nitrate in 170 litres (38 gals) of water. Note that a grade of calcium nitrate free from any ammonium salts must be used for this purpose. The quantity of calcium nitrate used should be reduced if calcium is present in the mains water supply.

3 Nitric Acid
A 2% solution of nitric acid is produced by diluting concentrated acid accordingly. Note that great care should be used in doing this and that concentrated acid should always be added to water and never the reverse.

Methods of Use

The stock solutions are placed alongside the nutrient sump of the installation and the pumps of the automatic controller are connected.

The pH of the circulating solution is first adjusted to 6.0 by the addition of nitric acid. This is effected by setting the controller to a pH reading of 6.0 and allowing the automatic injection of nitric acid until this value is reached, when the controller will stop injection.

Nutrients are then injected to bring the salt concentration to the desired level. Starting levels of salt concentration (cf) will vary with different crops and with the stage of growth. Taking tomatoes as an example it is normal to start with a cf reading of 2. This figure is therefore set on the controller and injection of nutrients will take place until this level is reached. During the initial build up of nutrients, the dosage pumps should be set to inject 2 volumes of the calcium nitrate solution to 1 volume of the 'Solufeed' F solution.

On reaching the desired level the dosage pump should be altered to pump equal volumes of the two nutrient solutions.

Removal of nutrients by the plants will result in a fall in the total salt concentration and consequent automatic injection by the controller to maintain the set level. Similarly the replacement of water will also result in the addition of acid and nutrients to maintain the pH and CF levels.

Subsequent operation of the controller is by raising and lowering the total salt concentration. The technique of operating the controller will vary from crop to crop and will be dependent on the stage of growth. As an overall guide, the higher salt concentrations will result in controlled growth whilst freer growth can be obtained by lowering concentrations. The general aim should be to operate at the lowest concentrations when maximum growth is desired.

Self-Formulated Feeds for Tomatoes, Cucumbers Mainly

It cannot be emphasized too strongly the ongoing stage of research into N.F.T. and companion systems of culture. Much of this centres around nutrient solutions which stay 'stable' for as long as possible and avoid mineral upsets in the growing plants. Typical in this respect is research at the West of Scotland Agricultural College who have evolved nutrient solutions based on the 'stable' premise. A precis of technical note 52 (West of Scotland Agricultural College), Hall, Wilson and Hutchison, January 1979 is given. This paper reiterates the nutrient needs of plants and quotes the macro nutrients as nitrogen, phosphorus, potassium, calcium, magnesium and sulphur and trace elements as iron, manganese, boron and zinc, copper, molybdenum and chlorine. It points out that these nutrients absorbed by plant roots from the solution as charged particles called *ions* in the forms of *cations* and *anions* and quotes it as a fundamental law that any solution containing ions must always have an equal number of positive and negative charges. In addition two other ions are formed from the water itself, namely hydrogen cations which cause low pH or acidity and hydroxl anions which give rise to high pH or akalinity. In neutral solutions there are equal numbers of hydrogen and hydroxyl ions. Nevertheless the rates of absorption of nutrients from the solution vary the number of cations and anions taken up. The main factor determining this is the ionic form of nitrogen which can be given either as an anion NO_3- or a cation NH_4+. Plants absorb both forms of this nitrogen rapidly and in large amounts and where the nitrogen supply is largely in cation form NH_4+ this will cause a *lowering* of the pH. Conversely when nitrogen is supplied as anions as NO_3- this will cause a *rise* in the pH.

It is stated in this paper that if the correct balance between NH_4+ and NO_3- nitrogen is provided, plants will absorb equivalent amounts of cations and anions. When using soft water, neutral ion uptake occurs when about 10–12% of the nitrogen is supplied in ammonium form.

The nutrient solutions formulated and used at the West of Scotland College *in relation to the water supply there* are as follows:

Nutrient element		Solution concentration (ppm)(mg/litre)
Potassium	K	300
Calcium	Ca	137
Nitrate nitrogen	N as NO_3-	96
Ammonium nitrogen	N as NH_4+	12
Phosphorus	P	67
Magnesium	Mg	46
Sulphur	S	162
Iron	Fe	5
Manganese	Mn	2
Boron	B	0.3
Copper	Cu	0.1
Zinc	Zn	0.1
Molybdenum	Mo	0.02

Preparation of Nutrient Solutions

It is an important matter when preparing nutrient solutions that the water supply be analysed. The college use an N.F.T. 'starter' solution as follows:

Fertilizer	g/100 litres	Nutrient concentration (ppm) (mg/litre)	
Calcium nitrate $Ca(NO_3)_2.4H_2O$	80.9	N 96;	Ca 137
Potassium sulphate K_2SO_4	55.4	K 249;	S 102
Potassium phosphate KH_2PO_4	17.7	K 51;	P 40
Ammonium phosphate $NH_4H_2PO_4$	9.9	N 12;	P 27
Magnesium sulphate $MgSO_4.7H_2O$	46.2	Mg 56;	S 60
Iron EDTA FeNaEDTA	3.27	Fe 5	
Manganese sulphate $MnSO_4.4H_2O$	0.02	Mn 2	
Boric acid H_3BO_3	0.172	B 0.3	
Zinc sulphate $ZnSO_4.7H_2O$	0.044	Zn 0.1	
Copper sulphate $CuSO_4.5H_2O$	0.04	Cu 0.1	
Ammonium molybdate $(NH_4)_6Mo_7O_{24}.4H_2O$	0.005	Mo 0.02	

Composition of Topping-Up Solution

Topping-up solution 1	Concentration (g/1)
Calcium nitrate $Ca(NO_3)_2.4H_2O$	80.9

Topping-up solution 2	
Potassium sulphate K_2SO_4	55.4
Potassium phosphate KH_2PO_4	17.7
Ammonium phosphate $NH_4H_2PO_4$	9.9
Magnesium sulphate $MgSO_4.7H_2O$	46.2
Iron EDTA FeNaEDTA	3.27
Maganese sulphate $MnSO_4.4H_2O$	0.82
Boric acid H_3BO_3	0.172
Zinc sulphate $ZnSO_4.7H_2O$	0.044
Copper sulphate $CuSO_4.5H_2O$	0.040
Ammonium molybdate $(NH_4)Mo_7O_{24}.4H_2O$	0.005

This whole principle of ion stabilization is one which must be pursued further by any grower wishing to use self-formulated feeds as opposed to the constant pH adjustment necessary with many other systems.

Self-Formulated Feeds for Lettuce N.F.T.*

	pH normal per litre	pH too high per litre (over 6.5)
Solution A		
Calcium Nitrate	264 mg	264 mg
Potassium Nitrate	354 mg	354 mg
Ammonium Nitrate	32 mg	32 mg
Solution B		
Fosmagnit	191 mg	109 mg
Sulphate of Potash	17 mg	17 mg
Magnesium Sulphate	37 mg	86 mg
Iron Chelate 330 Fe	50 mg	50 mg
Manganese Sulphate	1 mg	1 mg
Zinc Sulphate	0.25 mg	0.25 mg
Borax	1.6 mg	1.6 mg
Copper Sulphate	0.12 mg	0.12 mg
Soldium Molybdate	0.12 mg	0.12 mg
Solution C		
Phosphoric Acid (pH adjustment)	–	29 mg

(*Check local water supply)

It is usual to start with Solution A topping up with Solution B as demanded by adjustment of conductivity to around 2000 mhos (microsiemens) and pH6. Proprietary feeds can be used.

Rock Wool Systems for Plant Culture, Principally Tomatoes and Cucumbers

Rock wool is presently available in the U.K. as 'Grodan' (Brinkman Horticultural Services U.K. Limited, Dunswell Lane, Dunswell, Hull, North Humberside) and 'Rocksil' (Cape Insulation Limited, Rocksil Works, Stirling). Other suppliers are now developing. Suppliers of the liquid feeds referred to later are available from Brinkman's.

Part of the inert sterile growing medium syndrome of which much more will undoubtedly be heard in the next decade, rock wool systems have had considerable development in Holland, Denmark and more limited in the U.K., although it is a system gaining great favour in North Humberside. Basically speaking, rock wool substrates are a form of hydroponics but with no nutrient re-circulation and require almost as much attention to detail with appropriate monitoring of chemical solutions used as N.F.T. systems. The emphasis is again on pH and conductivity. Much research and practical growing work has been carried out at A.D.A.S. Stockbridge House Experimental Station, Cawood, Selby, North Yorkshire *and the notes which are given refer largely to their work*, but there is reference to research at other centres in Holland and elsewhere. A feature of rock wool culture in common with 'hydro cultural' systems of pot plants (perlite, etc.) is the need to grow plants from the outset in the chosen medium. This is not only for avoidance of fungal infection but because of the nature of roots which form as these react unfavourably to changes in substrate plant raising. It is therefore essential to use rock wool propagating blocks, the most common size being 7.5 cm cubes. Cucumbers can be sown directly into a slit in the top of this cube but for tomatoes it is normal to raise seedlings in some inert medium such as perlite and prick out into rock wool blocks. The blocks must be wet with the warmed nutrient solution before sowing or pricking out and are placed on polythene, being fed with the nutrient solution at each watering and spaced out as described under traditional plant raising with a watering system. In the tomato growing notes the layout of plants has been broadly described but more detail now follows.

Slabs of expanded polystyrene must be placed *beneath* the rock wool to prevent downward movement of heat. These slabs should be 5 cm thick at least and grooved out to accommodate 20 mm alkathene pipe above the slabs (see Figure 8). These pipes are run at a temperature of around 103°F (40°C) to keep the rock wool mat at about 74–77°F (23°–25°C). It may be necessary to have a separate take off from the boiler for this purpose.

Rock wool slabs are 3 ft × 1 ft × 3 in (90 × 30 × 7.5 cm) for cucumbers and 3 ft × 6 in × 3 in (90 × 15 × 7.5 cm) for tomatoes and

146 Nutrient Film Techniques and Rock Wool Systems

Figure 8 Rock wool system – typical lay-out

are placed end to end and wrapped in black/white polythene in threes to prevent movement of water and nutrients due to any slope. Nails are used to hold the polythene in place. These must *not* be galvanized, failing which use adhesive tape.

To set out the plants merely stand them on the growing slabs previously wetted with nutrients using one drip nozzle in each plant and at the outset letting the nozzles drip on to the rock wool slabs when the plants have been established. It may also be necessary to make slits in the side of the polythene to allow excess nutrients to drain off.

Nutrient Solutions
At the propagation stage a proprietary feed such as Nutriflora T is satisfactory and after planting two stock solutions are made up based on the analyses of the water supply as with N.F.T. Stockbridge House recommend two nutrient solutions be given alternately at each watering preferably through the conductivity meter. Further emphasis is made of the need to check the pH and conductivity of the solution in the

Nutrient Film Techniques and Rock Wool Systems 147

growing slabs, and the recommendation is that the pH should be between 6 and 6.5 and the conductivity 2,000 to 2,500 microsiemens for cucumbers and 2,500 to 3,000 for tomatoes. When the pH falls, stock solution 'B' is used and Fosmagnit is given in place of phosphoric acid. It will be necessary to vary the strength of the liquid feed to maintain the correct conductivity and, if this is too high, flushing out with fresh feed should reduce the salt levels, making a point of never flushing out with plain water. It is advisable to check the nitrogen, phosphorus, potassium, magnesium and calcium by analysis every 2–3 weeks and trace elements at 4 to 6 week intervals (see N.F.T.).

Mixing Feed Stock Solutions of X100 for Cucumbers and Tomatoes*

Quantities per 1,000 litres of water. This formula is for pure water and may need adjustment according to analysis of the water supply used.

Solution A

		Cucumbers	Tomatoes
Calcium nitrate	$Ca(NO_3)_2.H_2O$	63.7 kg	71.6 kg
Potassium nitrate	KNO_3	25.0 kg	25.0 kg
Ammonium nitrate	NH_4NO_3	4.0 kg	4.0 kg
Iron chelate 330 Fe	Fe–DTPA	560 g	560 g

Solution B

		Cucumbers	Tomatoes
Phosphoric acid 37%	H_3PO_4	21.2 litres	21.2 litres
Fosmagnit		8.9 litres	8.9 litres
Potassium sulphate	K_2SO_4	26.1 kg	26.1 kg
Magnesium sulphate	$MgSO_4.7H_2O$	12.8 kg	21.4 kg
Potassium nitrate	KNO_3	15.4 kg	15.4 kg
Manganese sulphate	$MNSO_4.H_2O$	160 g	160 g
Zinc sulphate	$ZNSO_4.7H_2O$	110 g	110 g
Borax	$Na_2B_4O_7.10H_2O$	180 g	180 g
Copper sulphate	$CuSO_4.5H_2O$	12 g	12 g
Sodium molybdate	$Na_2MoO_4.2H_2O$	12 g	12 g

Notes:
(i) Fosmagnit contains 12.4% P and 4.4% Mg.
(ii) Iron chelate Fe DTPA contains 9% Fe.
If Librel FeDP is used instead (6% Fe), substitute 840 g for 560 g in table.
*(Stockbridge House Recommendations.)

Chapter Sixteen

Plant Foods

The horticulturist knows that plants must have a supply of food if they are to grow. They must have a satisfactory diet and this means the whole spectrum of chemical elements, macro or major (required in large amounts), micro or minor (required in smaller amounts).

The bigger the demand on the plants in terms of size and crop yields the more plant food they require and of course different plants or even varieties of them have different diets, so it follows logically that where plants are grown under 'forced' conditions of protected culture they will invariably require a bigger diet. Basically speaking, 'short-term' crops (e.g. lettuce) are given all their food requirement at the outset (except for N.F.T. systems), while others (e.g. tomatoes) are given so much of their diet at the beginning (again except for any substrate system) and the rest regularly over their growing period. With N.F.T. or substrate systems different techniques are used but in essence the plant must still get its diet, albeit in a more precise form as there are no reserves of nutrients or 'buffering' of them as happens in the soil. The same is true of Aeroponic systems. Students of horticulture should be well versed in the detail of soil origins, nature and biological processes; if not they should refer to a suitable book on the subject (see book list, acknowledgements). Knowledge of the metabolic processes within the plant is also essential. For revision purposes a thumbnail sketch is given on some of the vital issues concerning plant nutrition.

Aeroponics

A new development for crops, involving mainly lettuce and bush-type tomatoes, is to grow them in polythene tubes. There is a 'platform' across the tube, which supports the plants.

A nutrient fog is circulated on a continuous basis around the roots and the foliage.

150 Plant Foods

Experience with this system seems so far confined to California, Holland, Israel and Italy.

Absorption

This is the taking in of water and soluble plant foods by the root or leaf of the plant. Water moves into the plant cell by osmosis when the stronger solution of salts in the cell pulls the water through the semi-permeable wall of the cell. The dissolved minerals move into the plant cell by a complicated base or ion (cations$^+$ and anions$^-$) exchange mechanism. Basically speaking the whole process of absorption depends much on osmosis and the concentrations of dissolved minerals in plant cell soil or substrate (peat, wood bark, straw, rock wool, perlite, etc.) not forgetting the strength of the nutrient solution. Where N.F.T. and substrates are concerned reverse osmosis can readily take place where the concentration of salts in the substrate or nutrient solution is too high (see transpiration and soil analysis).

Photosynthesis and Respiration

Air containing carbon dioxide gas (CO_2) at approximately 300 vpm is taken through the pores in the plant leaf cells where the presence of the green catalyst chlorophyll plus water and nutrients carbohydrate is synthesized and oxygen expelled. Respiration is the vital process for breathing carried out by all living organisms. Air is taken through pores or leaf stems and to a lesser extent roots and has its oxygen content extracted by various chemical processes and carbon dioxide expelled. A great deal depends on temperature and other vital factors, such as age and health of the plant. Growth is a continuous destructive process which uses up plant reserves which must be replaced by photosynthesis, so it is a finely balanced process much dependent upon day/night temperatures. This is why plants such as tomatoes can be thin and spindly after warm day/warm night; curled and over-vigorous after warm day/and cold night. Temperature control is a critical matter when aiming for maximum quality and yields.

Transpiration

Water taken in by roots passes through the plant where it is expelled as water vapour through leaf or stem pores. This process is much dependent on many factors, especially the humidity of the air as the humidity within the plant tends to balance itself with that of the atmosphere. There are many vital factors which control the transpiration, provided there is sufficient supply of moisture in the soil or substrate and this contains a satisfactory concentration of plant nutrients. Once again it is important that the plants have healthy roots and leaves, as disease can influence transpiration rate considerably.

Plant Foods 151

Translocation
Without going into detail this is a movement of 'materials' (basic minerals, manufactured foodstuffs, etc.) within the plant which is closely linked to the build-up or formation of protoplasm, the living material of the plant contained within the cell.

Metabolism
The building up and breaking down of compounds within the plant tissue can collectively be called metabolism. Various compounds may be found stored within the plant, e.g. carbohydrates in potatoes, nicotine in a tobacco plant, sugars in tomatoes, etc. The storage is for the benefit and intended use of the plant, not necessarily animal life, which includes us. The fact that we use these storage materials is coincidental to plant processes.

Other Functions
There are, in addition, all the innumerable functions such as germination, flowering, fruiting, seed production and many more, all tied up within the whole spectrum of plant growth. It is important to remember that, while it may be convenient to discuss plant processes and the main role of specific plant nutrients under headings, every process is interrelated in some way. It should also be remembered that plants are extremely sensitive to growing conditions and can react to them just as positively as we would do. There may be, if we can believe some plant physiologists, much reaction within plant life to external conditions, including sound, and our attitude to plants.

Groups of Nutrients
There are two main and one supplementary group of elements which in solution are necessary for plant growth –
1 *Major or Macro Nutrient Elements* required in large amounts (these are nitrogen, phosphorus, calcium, magnesium, potassium and sulphur). Also required are the 'gases' (oxygen, hydrogen and carbon dioxide).
2 *Trace, Micro or Minor Elements* required in small amounts, but still essential (iron, manganese, boron, copper, zinc, molybdenum).
3 Elements possibly of benefit to plant growth but not necessarily in the 'essential' category (sodium, chlorine, silicon, aluminium and a lot more).

Absorption by plants of all elements is only possible when they are in certain forms, e.g. nitrogen as nitrates or ammonium salts, phosphorus as phosphoric acid, calcium, magnesium and potassium as oxides, sulphates or chlorides, sulphur as sulphates, iron as ferric or ferrous salts, boron as borates, copper and zinc as their salts, molybdenum as molybdates.

152 Plant Foods

Note that absorption is
(a) Only possible if solutions are diluted (measured by their conductivity – see later).
(b) There is avoidance of antagonism which means too much of one element in relation to another.
(c) Taken up by the plant in balanced amounts relative to the stage of growth, type of plant, for varied conditions and so on, the pH of the solution of elements, substrate or soil correct for the species of plant concerned with the effect this has on micro-biological acticity, especially in soil.
(d) There is sufficient availability of oxygen in solutions, substrate or soil.
(e) Supplies of water and air are adequate, bearing in mind the plant's need for oxygen for breathing and carbon dioxide for photosynthesis.

Role of Function of Elements

Major Elements

Nitrogen
An important constituent of many vital materials contained in plants, especially in the growing parts (shoots, leaves, etc.) It is therefore required in large quantities by actively growing plants and, if deficient, plants will be stunted and pale. Nitrogen in certain forms is a very mobile element capable of quick movement or rapid movement to actively growing parts where required. For this reason, deficiency is more likely to occur in the older, less active parts of the plant where, in addition to stunting of growth generally, there is yellowing and paleness of leaf colour. Excess of nitrogen results in very soft leafy growth (see potassium).

Occurrence Factors
Waterlogging or lack of oxygen of soil or substrate quickly results in lack of nitrogen availability to the plant. Light soils lacking organic matter will quickly become deficient in nitrogen compared to good highly organic soils which 'hold' the nitrogen better.

Correction
In general, apply nitrogen but see respective Crop Notes.

Phosphorus
Phosphorus has many essential roles in plants, principally as a constituent of the cell nucleus and respiration generally so that its deficiency

results in restricted growth in every part of the plant including production of seed. Symptoms of deficiency are not unlike nitrogen deficiency, with drooping leaves and purple tints, along with restricted leaves. Excesses of phosphorus seldom manifest themselves due to the insoluble nature of phosphorus not in demand.

Occurrence Factors
Heavy, poor clay soils and substrates which are acid in nature (low pH.)

Correction
Adjust pH and apply phosphates, but see Crop Notes.

Calcium
Calcium is present in all plants as a constituent of the cell wall (calcium pectate). Calcium is not especially mobile in the plant which accounts for the reason that deficiency will result in die-back of growing shoots, in addition to side-effects such as die-back of tomato fruit trusses and black bottoms from the fruit (see Chapter 11). Calcium has of course a vital role relative to neutralization of the acid excretions resulting from micro-organism activity. Excess of calcium generally results in high pH with many side effects (see iron).

Occurrence Factors
Acid soils or substrates or soil containing a lot of sodium (such as salt water flooding), conditions of heavy watering or high rainfall out of doors can result in calcium deficiency, especially in light soil. Excess calcium is of course inevitable in areas overlying chalk.

Correction
Adjust pH by applying calcium or reduce pH by applying flowers of sulphur, but see Crop Notes.

Magnesium
This is a vital constituent of chlorophyll and any shortage manifests itself in the leaves producing brown, orange tints and severe interveinal chlorosis on the older leaves first, as magnesium is very mobile within the plant and will always be 'moved' to the vital growth areas.

Occurrence Factors
Frequently linked with calcium deficiency on light soils or very porous substrates. Also occurs, especially with tomatoes, when there is an excess of potash (see Chapter 11). Soils lacking in organic matter also give rise to magnesium deficiency especially under intensive cultural conditions.

Correction
See Crop Notes. Avoid excess application of magnesium because of its effect on the soluble salt content of the soil.

Potassium
Present in all plants in large amounts, especially rapidly growing fruit-bearing species, (e.g. tomatoes). Its role as a catalyst and water-movement controller is vital. It is very mobile and symptoms of deficiency tend to appear as marginal leaf scorch of the leaves first, but secondary issues such as blotchy ripening of tomatoes are a part of the potassium syndrome. Also highly important is the relationship between potassium and nitrogen, as potassium shortage can be closely linked to soft growth typical of nitrogen surplus, and vice versa. Indeed, many aspects of plant culture relate to the delicate balance between potash and nitrogen, especially a rapidly growing heavy-bearing crop such as tomatoes. Potassium levels can also affect the uptake of magnesium.

Occurrence Factors
Generally related under protected culture to lack of appreciation of potassium demands for crop concerned.

Correction
Pay strict attention to feeding programme for crop concerned; where excess potash occurs flood out during non-cropping periods, as far as this is practical.

Sulphur
Required by all plants as a constituent of chlorophyll. Deficiency symptoms similar to nitrogen shortage and exhibited on leaves but with much more elongation of shoots with no side shoot formation on soft crops. Deficiencies will seldom occur in a normal situation. Excesses are due to atmospheric industrial pollution. Faulty combustion of heating systems is much more likely, and this causes dead areas with soft leaves such as in tomatoes or cucumbers.

Trace (Micro or Minor) Elements

Iron
Very closely tied up with chlorophyll manufacture as a catalyst so any shortage quickly shows up as a yellowing or whitening of leaf, and not being mobile symptoms will show up first on younger leaves. Excesses of iron are unlikely to present great problems under 'normal' conditions, as the iron is rendered unavailable. Excess with N.F.T. solutions can cause considerable damage.

Plant Foods

Occurrence Factors
There can be many complex reasons why iron is unavailable to plants, as in soil it is seldom actually not present. Excesses of manganese, zinc, copper, cobalt, nickel, calcium, phosphorus and deficiencies of magnesium and phosphorus are reported as giving rise to iron deficiencies within the plant. It could be said that the availability if iron is a highly sensitive affair demanding critical appraisal of all nutrition programmes, although in practice high pH of nutrient solutions, soil or substrate, is the most frequent cause of its unavailability – this being called lime-induced chlorosis.

Correction
Lowering of pH by various means, such as adding flowers of sulphur to soil, is a somewhat drastic measure but can help to overcome lime-induced chlorosis in a difficult situation, as also can the addition of sphagnum peat with its low pH, while foliar application of sulphate or iron at 0.2 – 1% can be used for hard-leaf species (i.e. fruit trees). This method has little application for glasshouse crops, as it can damage leaves. pH correction or the use of iron chelates in liquid food is the most usual method of attacking the problem.

Manganese
This is closely linked with iron so also affects chlorophyll formations. Symptoms of deficiency are therefore similar, although there is more blotchiness or leaf curling. Symptoms of excess result in die-back of shoots and leaves.

Occurrence Factors
High pH, high organic matter with excess moisture. Excess can occur frequently when glasshouse soils are heat sterilized.

Correction
This can be done in several ways. First of all by checking pH or as a last resort spray with a 1–2% manganese sulphate solution, plus spreader. Many complete fertilizers are available which contain manganese. This also applies to liquid foods. Where toxicity occurs, flooding should be carried out where practicable.

Boron
The exact role of boron is not known, except that it acts as a catalyst for many vital processes. It seems tied up with calcium and can delay the onset of calcium deficiency but not replace it. Boron may also be involved in the regulation of potash/calcium ratios. Its shortage can

156 Plant Foods

result in the collapse of cell walls causing damaged shoots to die back and fruits to go corky, especially tomatoes.

Occurrence Factor
A shortage of boron is unlikely unless in certain soils or certain districts, where boron is lacking in the water supply. It is common where the pH goes too high.

Correction
It is essential to check water supplies for N.F.T. systems. Boron can readily be added to liquid feeds as Borax or Borate, at minimal dilution. Toxicity is more difficult to deal with, as it is very persistent in the soil. It is of course used as a base for weedkillers.

Zinc and Copper
Zinc and copper also act as catalysts and so cell collapse occurs if deficiency is acute.

Correction
Where zinc or copper deficiency is confirmed, it is safer to use a complete fertilizer containing these elements, as amounts needed by plants are very small. For N.F.T. systems check water supply and add or leave out as required.

Soil, Substrate, Solution and Tissue Analysis

Cultural practices under protection in the modern idiom with their high investment in manpower, fuel and equipment demand maximum returns if they are to be profitable.

All crop growth depends on the correct balance of light, heat, water and dissolved nutrients under any system of culture.

Plants are contrary things subject to many variables and cannot always be expected to perform predictably. This is especially so in the realm of nutrient absorption.

Much can, of course, be achieved by visual means, which after all is the first stage of all nutritional assessment.

The intuitive grower very quickly becomes sensitive to the plants' needs or surpluses by watching them grow, and this is especially true of the professional adviser who views crops even more objectively than the grower as he is able to compare growth across a range of crops.

Nevertheless, there is still a vital need for finding out what nutrient levels are available to the plants, *before* the crop commences, *during* growth, and if necessary what nutrients have actually been taken up by the plant. This is achieved by various forms of analysis, the more precise forms of which are laboratory performed.

All forms of analysis endeavour, basically by extraction or solvent methods and thereafter by colour comparison in various ways, electrical conductivity, and miscellaneous other methods, to show what elements are 'available' to the plant and in what strength of solution. Tissue analysis shows what the tissue actually contains.

Ministry of Agriculture Bulletin 27 gives an excellent description of the main laboratory procedures (Analysis of Agricultural Material).

Grower Analysis

Growers wishing to carry out self-analysis can do so with 'Sudbury' testing kits (Sudbury Technical Products Ltd., Corwen, Clwyd LL21 ODR). While not as accurate as laboratory analysis, 'Sudbury' kits are useful for 'on the spot' information.

Also available are pH meters (for measurement of exchangeable calcium) and conductivity meters which measure the conductivity of the soil solution, or more usefully liquid feeds. Both pH and conductivity meters are essential equipment for NFT cultural systems.

Some Aspects of Analysis

Organic Matter Levels

It is useful to know levels of organic matter in soil or compost. A figure of 8–12% is usual (including moisture) but some soils, especially those of a peaty nature, would have much higher levels. It is obvious that peat-based composts will have a very much higher organic matter level.

Lime

Knowing the pH of a soil, substrate or solution is one thing. How much calcium to add is another as soils vary a lot in their ability to absorb lime, or leave it 'free'. Most laboratories quote a lime requirement figure in cwts/acre or kg/ha to 6 in (15 cm) depth *ground limestone*, and this figure can readily be reduced to ozs per sq yd (or g per m^2). Calcium magnesium ratio is important for tomatoes and 10:1 is usual to help avoid blossom end rot.

Nitrogen

This is determined by ppm (mg/litre) nitrate, also index factors, 2–5, according to previous crop history and whether or not the soil is chemically or heat sterilized or has bulky organic matter applied. Normal figures for nitrogen are 50–150 ppm (mg/litre) nitrate in either soil, substrate or liquid solution.

Phosphorus
This is calculated on different extraction methods on the scale 0–280 ppm (mg/litre) P in soil (index 0–9) on sodium bicarbonate extraction or the scale (or 0–300 ppm (mg/litre) (index 0–9) on ammonium acetate/acetic acid extract). Index 3–5 is standard for most greenhouse crops. It can also be reported in mg per 100 g P_2O_5 stated as *low*, *medium* or *high*.

Potassium
This is reported in ppm (mg/litre) K in soil on ammonium nitrate extract 0–3, 600 (index 0–9) (or ammonium acetate/acetic acid extract 0–3,000, index 0–9).

Index 4–5 (405–900 ppm K and 355–700 ppm K) is standard for most greenhouse crops. It can also be reported in mg/100 g K_2O and stated as low, medium or high.

Magnesium
Reported generally on ammonium nitrate extract as ppm (mg/litre) mg in soil the scale is 0–1,500 (index 0–9). Indices in the 3–5 range are normal but ratio of magnesium to potassium is important. Calcium to magnesium rate of around 10/1 is critical with many crops.

Soluble Salts pC (Potential Coefficient)
This is a measure of soil conductivity. A.D.A.S. (Agricultural Development Advisory Service) do this on the saturated calcium sulphate technique ranging from 1,900–4,010 mhos (microsiemens) (index 0–9). Indices around 3–4 are usual. Other laboratories calculate on pC scales, safe levels being 2.8–3.00. Other methods are in use. The comparison is as follows:
A.D.A.S. Scales: index 3–4 (2,610–2,800) CF 16–10 = pC 2.8–3.00 mhos (microsiemens)

Balance of Main Nutrients
What is often more important than actual quantities available is the balance of the main nutrients to each other and this varies with different crops.

Tissue Analysis
This is a task primarily for the well-equipped laboratory. Discs are now available for a quick determination of leaf content.

Eelworm Determination
A count of 'live' eelworm cysts (those containing live larvae of *globodera rostochiensis*) is highly desirable for all land intended for tomato culture.

Taking Samples for Analysis

Representative samples in the area of crop are essential, usually taken with an auger or trowel at 5–6 in (12.5–15 cm) depth or from stock piles. These are bulked and a 2 lb (around 800 g) sample extracted, clearly labelled and despatched to a laboratory, or air dried for self-analysis.

Weeds, Pests and Diseases

Previous crop history and observations are key issues but much can be determined by physical examination, bottle/tray tests in warm regions, etc. Culture experiments with quick seedlings, such as cress, to check for residual chemicals (such as Basamid, etc.) are also useful. Sterilization should always be the rule if in doubt (see page 164) about pests and diseases.

A Practical Approach to Liquid Fertilizers

One has to return to 'olden' days to find reference to the supply of crops with all their plant food needs at the outset under protected cropping systems.

'Hot bed' enthusiasts were insistent on this 'once and for all' philosophy, the foundation of which was vast supplies of organic manure. To a lesser extent the same was true of soil- (and manure-) based composts where most if not all the plant's diet was included at potting stage.

When feeding was needed it so often took the form of a scatter of fertilizer, usually organic, which eventually was flushed in by watering. As far as crop culture is concerned, fertilizers in solid form are still used as bases and top dressings; indeed, base feed application is still a vital part of crop culture in borders, pots or containers.

Nowadays, apart from initial supplies of plant foods, it is the practice to meter out plant foods to crops in soluble form, called liquid feeding, the important issue being the *quantity* and *dilution* rate of the solution. The liquid feed may be applied in a variety of ways, by hand dilution and hand application, by hand dilution and application through spray lines, trickle systems, capillary matting, flood or flow benches, or by any practical means. It may also be diluted 'automatically' following addition of the raw material (e.g. the concentrated fertilizer to the diluting appliance). These vary from displacement to capillary tube type, dilutors to automatic injectors – everything being controlled by instruments provided by specialists and suppliers. These are mainly used for N.F.T. systems (see also Aeroponics, page 149).

Plant Foods

Dilution Strength
Plants have inbuilt characteristics which enable them only to extract *water* by osmosis and absorb *nutrients* when the dilution of soil or substrate is 'in tune' with the type of plant *and* its stage of growth, e.g. not supply a 'baby' plant with an 'adult' diet.

Nutrient Content
The balance and range of nutrients is highly important, relating this to crop type and state of growth, following visual assessment or analysis, usually both.

Proprietary Feeds
A wide range of these is available from a number of manufacturers for specific crop needs. They are used according to directions, either directly diluted if liquids, or if powder prepared in stock solutions for further dilution. Self-mixes involve buying 'straight' chemicals and first preparing stock solutions, then diluting.

Dilution Strength and Nutrient Contents
This is invariably stated as parts per million (ppm) or more recently mg/litre) following dilution at various rates, both factors dependent on the chemical used and *its* percentage.

There are several ways of going about things, most of which seem at the outset to be a little complicated. It is all tied up with weights and volumes, and this is a matter somewhat 'complicated' by metrication at the outset for the 'older' generation.

Stage 1

Imperial related to metric		weight/volume
1 Imperial pound (1 lb)	=	16 oz
1 Imperial gallon of *clean* water weighs 10 lbs	=	160 oz
1 Imperial pound	=	454 g
1 Imperial ounce	=	28.34 g

Note: difference between Imperial (British) and American gallons (1 British gallon = .83 U.S.A. gallon).

On Metric Calculations

1 cc of water	=	1 g

which is a very convenient measure as it is 1 g per million cubic centimetres of water.

Parts per million concept
This applies to the *actual quantities of chemical element in dilution*.
1 ppm could be 1 oz in 1,000,000 oz of water
      which is 1 oz in 62,500 lb of water
      or 1 oz in 6,250 gallons of water
      So
100 ppms is 100 oz in 1,000,000 oz of water
        or 100 oz in 6,250 gallons of water
        or 1 oz in 625 gallons of water
and
200 ppms is 200 oz in 1,000,000 oz of water
        or 200 oz in 62.50 gallons of water
        or 2 oz in 625 gallons of water
        or 1 oz in 31.20 gallons of water

When it is metric

1 ppm = 1 g in 1,000,000 ml or cc of water = 1 g in 1,000 litres of water (218 gallons) or 1 mg per litre – which is a very simple calculation indeed.
   100 ppm = 100 g/1,000 litres = 100 mg/litre
   200 ppm = 200 g/1,000 litres = 200 mg/litre

Stage 2
But chemicals are seldom 100% pure and only contain a percentage of actual nutrient.
  So let us start again.

    1 oz in 1,000,000 oz = 1 ppm
    1 oz of a 20% fertilizer in 625 gallons becomes only 20% strength, so instead of being 1 ppm it is only 20% – $\frac{1}{5}$th of a ppm = 0.2 ppm
    so, to keep it at 1 ppm, 5 times the amount would be required = 5 oz.

    And in metric

    It must also be 5 g per 1,000 litres (5 mg/litre) to be 1 ppm of the actual element.

Stage 3
Nutrients are seldom only *one* element and usually N, P and K, so this applies for each nutrient.

    A 20% N.P.K. fertilizer used at 5 oz per 62.50 gallons (or 5 mg/litre) becomes 1 ppm N, 1 ppm P and 1 ppm K

Stage 4

Correctly speaking, the way to proceed *exactly* is to first calculate molecular weight, e.g. sulphate of ammonia = $(NH_4) SO_4$ from molecular weight tables.

$(2 \times 14) + (2 \times 4) + 32 + (4 \times 16) = 132$

percentage nitrogen container is

$\frac{(2 \times 14)}{132} \times 100 = 21.3\%$ N

percentage *salt* (or fertilizer) required to any ppm is as follows:
For 180 ppm (mg/litre)

$\frac{180}{21.3} \times 100 = 845$ g

so that 845 g salt is needed to give 180 ppm in 1,000 litres (mg/litre).

Fertilizers Frequently Used for Liquid Feeding

Ammonium Nitrate	35% N
Nitrate of Potash	13% N 46% K_2O
Calcium Nitrate	11.9% N 16.9% Ca
Mono-ammonium Phosphate	12% N 16.5% P_2O_5
Magnesium Sulphate	9.9% Mg

By the same token, as 1 ppm equals 1 lb in 100,000 gallons = 845 lb in 100,000 gallons (1,000,000 lb) this is in more mundane terms .845 lb (13½ oz) in 100 gallons. This still gives the same dilution rate at 180 ppm N.

At a *very rough* calculation:

> 1 lb per 100 gallons of 20% N, 20% P and 20% K would give – 1 in 1,000,

but only 20% of fertilizer is actual element, so it becomes

> 200 ppm N, P and K

In metric terms

> 1 kg of 20–20–20 fertilizer in 1,000 litres would give 200 ppm N, P and K (mg/litre)

Fertilizers are, however, seldom diluted in bulk. Stock solutions are made up with *warm* water (to dissolve salts) and should be warm enough to prevent solidification (above 50–54°F/10–12°C).

They are diluted at various rates according to formulae, at which dilution they have a satisfactory salt content (pC or CF) not damaging to plants.

Lowering the dilution rate requires more water – raising it, less. The following table shows standard type feeds:

1. Liquid Feeds with Nitrogen and Potassium Fertilizers

Liquid feed $N:K_2O$	Oz/gal and grams[+] per litre of stock solution				ppm (mg/litre) in 1/200 dilution	
	Nitrate of potash		Ammonium nitrate		N	K_2O
	oz/gal	g/l	oz/gal	g/l		
2:0:1	10	65	23	149	300	150
1:0:1	18	114	17	109	260	260
1:0:1.5	24	156	12	80	240	360
1:0:2	28	179	8	52	205	410
1:0:2.5	31	196	4	31	180	450
1:0:3	35	224	2	15	170	515
1:0:3.5	41	261	–	0	170	600

[+]Grams per litre = 1 g in 1,000 g which equals 1 lb per 100 gallons (1,000 lb)

2. Liquid Feeds Supplying Nitrogen, Phosphorus and Potassium

Liquid Feed Nutrient ratio $N:P_2O_5:K_2O$	Oz/gal and grams per litre of stock solution						ppm (mg/litre) in 1/200 dilution		
	Nitrate of potash		Mono-ammonium phosphate		Ammonium nitrate		N	P_2O_5	K_2O
	oz/gal	g/l	oz/gal	g/l	oz/gal	g/l			
2:1:1	10	65	7	48	20	131	300	150	150
2:1:2	17	110	6	41	14	91	250	125	250
2:1:3	24	155	6	39	10	66	240	120	360
2:1:4	29	186	5	35	6	42	215	108	430
2:1:5	31	198	4	30	3	21	180	90	450
1:1:1	17	110	13	82	12	76	250	250	250
1:1:2	29	183	10	68	4	29	210	210	420
1:1:3	38	241	9	60	–	0	195	185	555

Soil Sterilization

Soil and growing media sterilization or (more accurately) 'pasteurization' is by no means the modern technique it is often thought to be.

Modern methods are one thing but the basic philosophy another. One can find reference to 'partial sterilization' of soil by heat and chemicals many years ago, along with using chemicals not so far removed from those used today, including volatile hydrocarbons, tar acids (carbolic and cresol), formalin, calcium sulphide, etc.

Excellent accounts of the work carried out by Russell and Fetherbridge appeared in the Journal of the Board of Agriculture over the years 1912–1914. Both steam and dry heat were used in much the same way as today. Ancient horticulturists were also well aware of the implications of 'soil sickness' and had various methods of overcoming it using chemicals and other means. There appears to be little place for satisfactory rotation of border grown crops except under mobile structures and even this has long-term problems. *Complete* sterilization is not desirable with soils as this would give rise to loss of fertility and other side issues. Basically, what is required is to free the soil as effectively as possible of its ills (pests, diseases, weeds), and reduce soil sickness problems generally, leaving behind the beneficial bacteria and fungi.

Depth of effective sterilization of border soil is always a problem and many growers have given up trying to control deep-seated virus or eelworm problems and gone on to alternative cultural systems (Growbags, N.F.T., etc.).

Sterilization by Heat

The object is to bring the soil as quickly and uniformly as possible to a temperature which will destroy harmful organisms. Many weaker parasites are destroyed in the range of 130–150°F (54–66°C), whereas others, such as virus disease and eelworms, require over 200°F (92°C).

There is no point in over-sterilizing soil as it can encourage formation of toxic substances and destroy physical texture too, if dry heat is used, by 'burning off' organic matter.

Methods of Sterilization by Heat

While there are a great many ways of applying heat to growing media, economics must be considered.

Hoddesden Grid Method

Developed at Hoddesden, Herts, where at that time the Cheshunt Research Station was located, perforated pipes are dug into the soil at 12 in (30 cm) depth around 18 in (45 cm) apart. The length of the pipes, usually 1¼ in (3.5 cm) diameter, will depend on the output of steam, as also will size of the 'main' from the boiler. The effective quantity of steam at the grid is around 18 lb/ sq ft per hour (90 kg/m^2). The calculation is as follows:

e.g. output of boiler 1,000 lb/steam per hour (453 kg per hour)

$$\text{so } \frac{1,000}{18} = 60 \text{ sq ft of border}$$

$$\text{or, in metric terms } \frac{453}{90} = 5.5 \text{ m}^2$$

Length of pipes at 18 in (45 cm) output will be 40 ft (12 m) with a 1¼ in (32 mm) main. With larger boilers, 'main' size is as follows:

Boiler Pressure
(5–15 p.s.i. – 3 in main) 0.3 – 1 bar (35–100 kN/m^2) – 75 mm main
(15–25 p.s.i. – 2 in main) 1 – 2 bar (105–175 kN/m^2) – 50 mm main
(25–60 p.s.i. – 1 in main) 2 – 4 bar (175–420 kN/m^2) – 40 mm main
(60–120 p.s.i. – 1¼ in main) 4 – 8 bar (420–840 kN/m^2) – 32 mm main

Soil should be fairly dry and well cultivated, especially at lower depths, avoiding a 'panned' condition.

Digging in the grids usually follows a pattern, and the soil is well firmed over the grids, and a PVC sheet used to cover the steamed area, and two sets of grids used to allow continuous steaming.

Steam is applied until the top 1 in (2.5 cm) of soil reaches 190–200°F (88–93°C), the usual period is 20–25 minutes per area.

Labour per acre is 500–600 man hours and, with fuel quantities of 2,500 gallons (23,000/ha), the high costs have practically ruled out grid steaming except on the smaller holdings.

Steam 'Plough'
Where there are modern greenhouses free from 'floor' obstruction, steam ploughs winched through well-cultivated soil reduce labour by 70–80%. Details are available from suppliers. More designs are now available.

Sheet Steaming
Developed originally in Holland and taken up by H. B. Wright of Cottingham (Humberside), this involves steam being introduced under PVC sheets, held down by soil, chains or sand-filled old fire hose. The steam is distributed through a box perforated with holes, often called a 'coffin'.

It is important to balance steam volume with area steamed. A 1,000 lb per hour steam boiler will, with a 1¼–1½ steam main, deal with an

166 Plant Foods

area of around 800 sq. ft at a pressure of 60–100 p.s.i. (450 kg/h boiler with 32–40 mm main will steam 75 m^2 at a pressure of 4–6.5 bar).

Penetration of steam depends on soil type and moisture content, so soil should be openly cultivated and not too wet or dry. Heat moves down by heat interchange. It can take a considerable time to achieve sufficient depth for deep-rooted crops and the technique is more popular with lettuce and chrysanthemums or flower growers.

Thermometers (thermo couple type) should be inserted obliquely from the side of the steamed area to check that at least 160°F (71°C) has been achieved. Steam traps are used to keep steam dry.

Modifications of the system to avoid over-sterilization of the top surface include the introduction of air (National Institute Agricultural Engineering, Silsoe, Beds., Occasional Note No. 99) and use of nets over the PVC to allow extra pressure of steam under sheet.

Low Pressure Steam

Full details of 'low pressure' steam sterilizers will be found in W.J.C. Lawrence Books and others (see Acknowledgements). They involve a layer of soil on perforated trays over trays of water. Commercial forms of this low pressure sterilizer were made, some wheeled. Low pressure sterilization is only useful on small scale and soilless composts have largely ousted their economic viability. Checks of temperature are essential.

Rotary Drum Sterilizer

Soil is rotated round a metal drum and falls through a fierce flame. The angle of the drum determines how many times the soil passes the flame and some adjustment is necessary to ensure that the soil is not over- or under-sterilized by checking the temperature of the ejected soil. Here again, these units are only practical on a smaller scale and their high labour content makes them less viable in modern terms.

Electric Sterilizers

Various forms of these, which operate on the panel element system, are available and are both useful and efficient on limited scale operation. Soil must not be too dry or it is liable to over-sterilization.

Other Heat-dependent Methods

Boiling water applied to limited areas, hot plates and other methods may still be used with some effect but only for small-scale operations.

Chemical Sterilization

Note: The following is a full account of chemicals available and those used today (1982): Despite the use of soilless composts, disease-resistant cultural or root-stocks, grow bags, rock wool, straw bales and other systems divorced from soil, there still remains a vast amount of crop production in borders. It is not always economically viable to sterilize by heat, especially when capital spending is involved for the purchase of equipment which will have very limited use. This is why in recent years chemical sterilization has become almost the 'accepted' way of sterilization. The ranges of chemicals used have varying effectiveness but are, if applied correctly, highly efficient, noting their limitations in certain instances for specific troubles.

Soil Preparation

The first priority is that the soil or growing media is well cultivated, neither wet nor dry, and most important, is at the correct temperature. There are, in theory, two basic types called *Contact* – applied in large volumes – and *Fumigant* – which is applied in small quantities and forms gas which moves through the soil or media. It is in practice difficult to differentiate between the virtues of the two types, as gaseous fumes are concerned with both.

Cress Testing

It is advisable to check whether soil is free from chemicals by cress testing.

Formaldehyde

Available mainly as a 40% solution, it is mixed in water at 2 gallons per 100 gallons (2 litres per 100 litres) for washing down greenhouses, where it is applied forcibly, wearing protective clothing and masks, and to soils where it will control some fungal disorders but has little effect on eelworms or insects.

Soil after cultivation is also thoroughly drenched at 5–6 gallons per sq yd (27–32 litres/m^2). Soil or media should be above 40°F (5°C) and preferably higher.

Seek advice before using neat formalin for greenhouse fumigation

Formaldehyde is still widely used for 'mild' troubles. 'Jeyes Fluid', 'Sterizal', 'Armillotox' and other various chemicals involving cresylic acid and phenols in different formulations do not have Ministry of Agriculture approval for sterilization purposes.

The author is well aware that these and other products are widely sold and used but is not in any position to comment on their efficiency. Trial and error is the only course of action open to the grower.

Chloropicrin

This is a poison gas, best applied by contractors. It is less popular than Methyl Bromide (see page 169).

168 Plant Foods

It is applied at 540 lb or 33 gallons/acre (605 kg or 370 litres/ha) or by injection ⅛ fl oz at 8 in depth 12 in intervals (3.5 ml – 20 cm deep – 30 cm intervals). Soil temperature should be at least 50°F (10°C) and a period of 6–8 weeks should elapse before using soil or media. It controls a wide range of diseases, weeds and eelworm (*not* root knot eelworm). Mixtures of Chloropicrin with Dichloropropene + Dichloropropane and Methylisothiocyanate (MIT) may also be used at 25–45 gal/acre (281–506 litres/ha) with a wider spectrum of control (including root knot eelworm). *The same precautions and wait period applies.* It is applied with special equipment.

Dichloropropene and Dichloropropene + Dichloropropane (DD)
Used widely at one time by itself for eelworm control, this material is not now so popular due to its 'lingering' nature as it is a 'heavy' gas. Dichloropropene mixture is used at 400 lb or 33 gallons/acre (448 kg or 370 litres/ha) best injected with a gun at exactly the same rate and method as Chloropicrin (above). Dichloropropene itself is used at lower rates. A wait period of 6–10 weeks is necessary.

Metham Sodium
Various brands of this are available. While they can be injected into the soil or media and sealed in they are usually applied as a drench 1 gallon in 200 gallons water (1.5 litres in 100 litres) at 5 gallons/sq yd (2.7 litres/m^2) by hose or spray lines *using protective clothing and goggles.* It must be cultivated 'out' and a 10-week wait period is usual. *Do a cress test.* It has a wide spectrum of control (see chart, page 169).

Dazomet or Basamid
This is a powder or granular form of metham sodium now widely used for soil sterilization. It is rotavated into the soil at low speed to 8 in (22.5 cm) depth, the usual rate being 340 lb/acre (380 kg/ha) but this rate can be varied. After application it is 'sealed' in by watering or covered with polythene. It changes to gas according to temperature which should preferably be around 50°F (18°C). (It does operate at lower temperatures.) Soil or media must be cultivated on several occasions to release the gas after 6–8 weeks, but cress tests again are advisable.

Dazomet has an excellent spectrum of control and has widespread use both outdoors and under protection; while it can be contractor applied in both instances if desired, it is easily and safely self-applied.

Nabam (Dithiocarbamate) (Dithane A40)
This fungicide is used for various purposes, one of which is as a soil/media sterilant. It is diluted at 1 lb – 100 gallons (1 g/litre) and soil/

media thoroughly drenched at 5 gallons per sq yd.

It acts principally against brown root of tomatoes and phoma rot of chrysanthemums but would appear to have a wider spectrum of control in practice.

Organic soils are not effectively treated – soil/media can be replanted after 2–3 weeks.

Methyl Bromide

This gas is poisonous and must be contractor applied (or by qualified, trained people). (Restrictions may be pending.) It is very widely used today because of ease of application and the wide range of troubles controlled. Indeed trials have shown it to be as good as, if not better in some instances than steam. Rates of application depend on what problems exist (also soil type) but are on the following scale:

Minimum 1 lb/100 sq ft (normal troubles)   48 g/m^2
Medium 2 lb /100 sq ft   97 g/m^2
Maximum 3 lb/100 sq ft (severe weeds, etc.)   144 g/m^2

It is applied from gas containers or canisters under polythene sheets raised 8 in (20 cm) at least above ground to allow the gas to spread. Soil should not be too wet or dry (60% field capacity), with soil/media temperature *not* below 50°F (10°C). Compost can be treated in shallow heaps. Soil or media can be used in 7–10 days or less, doing a cress test if time allows. Confined areas must be freely ventilated before entering.

Economics

It is impossible to quote useful facts and figures for soil sterilization because of the changing scene. Growers are acutely conscious of sterilization costs, especially in view of alternative cultural systems, so it is a question of balancing the one against the other at actual costs, taking into account previous history of cropping and 'risk' factors for crop, e.g. high investment in fuel and labour.

Effectiveness of Sterilants Against Soil-Borne Pests and Diseases of Protected Crops*

Chemical	Rhizoctonia	Wilt diseases†	Phytophthora	Brown root rot	Potato cyst eelworm	Root knot eelworm	Free living eelworm	Pythium	Weeds	Insects	Interval between treatment and planting
+Formaldehyde+ Chrloropicrin	xx –	xx xxx	xx x	x x	– xxx	x x	x xx	xx x	x xx	– x	3–6 weeksø 4–8 weeksø
+Dichloropropene x Dichloropropane with Dichloropropane	–	–	–	x	xx	xxx	xx	–	–	–	At least 6 weeksø
+Metham-sodium or +Dazomet	xx	–	xx	xx	xxx	xx	xx	xx	xx	xx	Up to 10 weeksø
+Chloropicrin with Dichloropropane-Dichloropropene and Methylisothiocyanate +Nabam	x	xx	xx	xx	xxx	xxx	xxx	xx	xx	xx	At least 6 weeksø
	–	–	x	x	–	–	–	x	–	–	2 weeksø
Methyl Bromide	x++	xx+	xxx++	xx++	xxx+	xxx+	xxx+	xxx++	xxx	xx	7 daysø
Steam	xx	xx	xxx	xxx	xxx	xx	–	xxx	xxx	xxx	None

x = some control
xx = moderate control
xxx = good control

++ at 73 g sq m (1½ lb/100 sq ft)
+ at 98 g sq m (2 lb/100 sq ft)
ø dependent on soil and air temperature

*Summary information from Ministry of Agriculture Fisheries and Food, Short Term Leaflet 177

Chapter Seventeen

Composts

Propagation – Seed and Potting Composts

So much has been said and written about composts and so many formulae are available that one could almost be back at the pre-John Innes stage, when there was a 'special' compost for each group of plants. The trend in the past decade has been to move away from soil-containing composts to those based on peat. Basically speaking, there are still three main aspects to consider:
(1) Physical texture
(2) Nutrient supplies (and lack of toxic chemicals)
(3) Freedom from pests, diseases and weeds.

(1) Physical Texture
This relates to the air/moisture relationship. This is such an important issue, it is the reason why such a miscellany of composts is around, as pore space between the compost particles is vital. Roots will form and grow and the plant obtain its food at an optimum level *only* when the ideal air/water temperature balance is achieved for the particular species of plant involved.

The situation is a changing one according to season, age of plant and many other related issues, so it can be difficult to find the ideal formulae under all circumstances.

Physical Components of Compost for Plant Growth.

Peat
There are many different types and grades of peat – the differences relating to age, origin (type of surface growth before decomposition), water source, and other factors.

Composts

Ideally, well-structured brown-'celled' sphagnum moss peat is what to aim for if purchasing peat for compost mixing. Compost suppliers will tend to use this. Some mixing of peat types does not go amiss – including sedge peat (especially for blocking) or some of the blacker types of well-decomposed peat – provided there is not enough of this to upset air/water balance. Trace element supply to plants is helped by black peat.

Peats do vary a lot however – and firms specializing in peat for composts or specialized purposes undertake very considerable research into physical and chemical characteristics. How it is lifted and handled is important also, to avoid damage to cell structure. Also whether it is frozen or not (which shatters the 'cells'). Important factors are acidity (pH 3.5–4.5 for sphagnum), total organic matter, waxes, tannins, cellulose, lignins, nitrogen, pore space, water-holding capacity and many other characteristics, which affect the behaviour of the peat. There is a lot to be said for small-scale trial before going too far with one particular source of supply. A *good* peat is practically sterile and free from weeds.

Sand or Grit

While peat alone may be used for composts, sand or grit can be valuable for improving structure of the peat – or put another way making up for any deficiencies in the structure of the peat (or soil where that is used). The nature of sand is important. It should be clean, chemically inert, sharp (not rounded) – not contaminated with clay, silt, calcium or organic matter. Size of grain should be 60–70%, $1/8 - 1/16$th in (3mm – 1.5 mm). The fine sands recommended by the University of California in their manuals should be avoided in temperate zones – and probably in warmer climates too. There is virtue in varying sand size according to peat. If the peat is fine use a coarser sand and vice versa. The sand should be dry to facilitate mixing. If clean, it will require no sterilization. If the sand has a high pH, reduce the lime added to the compost. This can be quickly checked by B.D.H. indicator fluid and barium sulphate or pH meter (or soil testing kit).

Soil or Loam

It is because good loam complying to laid-down specifications can be difficult and expensive to obtain and require sterilization by heat or other means that soilless composts have become so popular. A good loam should contain clay 7–27%, silt 28–50% and less than 52% sand. It should also contain organic matter derived from grass roots. This means it is ideally stacked turf lifted from a pasture field and rotted down. The pH should also be adjusted to 6.3 before mixing by adding calcium carbonate. Most growers using soil would tend to select a suitable field supply but firms specializing in loam supplies *may* go through the accepted procedure of stacking 4½ in (10–11 cm) turves 6 ft (1.8 m) high in spring or early summer, interlaced with manure and lime in alternate layers before stripping down by spade – a costly procedure these days. The 'feel' of a loam – not too greasy or too light and gritty – is important. Ideally 'medium' loam is the best. Loam is bound to vary greatly and this, plus all the problems of effective sterilization, has swung many growers away from it. Nevertheless the 'buffer' qualities of a loam (its ability to hold reserves of plant foods, moisture, etc.) make it an attractive component of a compost.

Other Materials

Lignite
Supplies of lignite or brown coal are available throughout the world. It is an organic material with massive base exchange capacity. It is available in the U.K. from Devon (Watts Blake Bearne & Co. Ltd., Park House, Newton Abbot, Devon TQ12 4PS). The use of lignite as a compost 'stabilizer' will undoubtedly increase.

Leca
This blown-up clay is used mainly as a substrate for pot plants on sub-irrigation systems and not as a compost additive.

Wood Bark
Shredded and properly composted soft wood bark has made some impact into the compost sphere in recent years. With shortages of peat, wood bark is likely to be much more widely used, but it must be composted for 3 months or more, or nitrogen shortage is a problem.

Vermiculite
This mined mineral expands when subjected to intense heat and presents a large water-absorbing surface area, so it is very useful as a compost additive to about 10% by volume, but cost is a factor which must be taken into account. It contains magnesium, calcium and potassium.

Perlite
(Silvaperl Products Ltd., PO Box 8, Harrogate, Yorks HG2 8JW)
Heat-treated volcanic ash, blown up to a light fluffy material with a large surface area. This is an inert material which is being widely used as a compost additive throughout the world. Because it is used for insulation etc. in the building industry, it is readily available at reasonable cost but not necessarily well graded. It has been found to give an excellent air/moisture balance, used either by itelf on hydroponic sys-

tems or as a compost additive at various rates, according to purpose. It is a superb way of making up for physical deficiencies in other materials in a compost (e.g. poor peat or soil).

Sewage Sludge
Treated sludge including 'Polder' soil is being used as compost, especially for 'blocking' (peat blocks).

Plastics
Various 'waste' materials from the plastic industry are available, including shredded polystyrene, polyurethane, etc., and are said to increase temperature of compost because of insulation properties, improve air/moisture balance, etc. Study of various reports makes interesting reading and if supplies of shredded plastic are readily available they should be considered, after checking that they are not contaminated. Light reflection is a useful feature of these materials if used on the surface of pots or beds. Polyurethane blocks are also available.

Urea Formaldehyde
These foams have some use in composts or by themselves, but presently are considered too costly. Processed waste paper is also being investigated. Undoubtedly other materials will continue to make impact as a compost additive or substrate. Mineral rock wool (see Chapter 15) is a typical example of the latter. In addition, there are a great many other additives or substrates under scrutiny around the world – low cost and consistency being key issues.

'Prepared' Substrates
This includes products such as Jiffy Pots – compressed peat from Finland (Vapo blocks), etc.

(2) Nutrient Supply
A seed germinating or a cutting forming roots is not concerned with nutrient supply from outside sources. Seeds have an inbuilt store of food to carry them through the first stage of becoming self-supporting. When these internal reserves have been utilized, the plant then looks for a ready supply of the complete spectrum of plant foods *at the right concentration at the correct balance* for the time of year, prevailing temperature, etc. As the plant develops its appetite increases and it generally needs a greater supply of nutrients, but this varies with species.

Nutrient Release
Chemical firms have also been at some pains to evolve formulations of nutrients suitable as compost additives – this applies especially to those

of a slow release nature, resin or polyethelene coated and otherwise. 'Slow release' is the ideal concept for a compost, plant foods being *gradually* released without 'surge' or 'repression' in a form available to plants. They must also be reasonably stable to allow storage of the compost. A time limit may be imposed and *storage temperatures are important*. Soil-based composts contain clay fractions which absorb plant nutrients and release these to the plants on a base exchange basis. The clay particle surface is the seat of such exchange, where the nutrients held on the clay particle surface by electrical discharge (anions and cations) are taken in by the plant root to be replaced from reserves within the clay particle. Soilless composts of any type operate on a different principle in terms of nutrient release. They act like a sponge and absorb the dissolved plant nutrients, 'holding' this until taken in by the plant. This they will continue to do until the nutrients are exhausted.

(3) Pest, Diseases and Weeds

Freedom from pests, diseases and weeds is a vital issue for intensive growers. Use of peat-sand mixes and other sterile materials has reduced the need for sterilization by heat or chemical means.

Sterilization of Soil (See Chapter 16)

Where necessary, if steam sterilization can be performed it is ideal. Bins with perforated pipes set in their base are frequently used for soils. A 'link' to outside for delivery is a labour-saving facility which can be incorporated. Rotary drum sterilization is still widely practised. Chemical sterilization involves complicated soil handling if it is to be fully effective for composts.

The Compost Situation (1982)

These facts are well known to all discerning growers and students but the problem is to translate these various issues into practical fulfilment. This involves making positive decisions, taking the time of year into account with the lower nutrient demands of plants in winter. Cost factor is important too (see page 176). Research has taken place throughout the world by universities, research stations, commercial firms concerned with compost manufacture and chemical firms. Growers themselves have undertaken considerable investigation into compost formulation, using peat, soil, wood bark, sand, etc. Blocking compost is also the subject of much research. In addition, one cannot overlook the 'synthetic' compost sphere involving a number of materials such as rock wool, urea formaldehyde foam, shredded polyurethane, polystyrene, perlite, vermiculite, leca (expanded clay) and many more materials at the development stage. There is undoubtedly a conflict of principles between educational and research establishments seeking knowledge, and commercial firms motivated by profit. Yet few firms would be willing to risk their good name and possibly more without first undertaking very considerable and costly research. But mistakes can and do happen.

Selection of Compost Type
There can be no one answer to compost selection. So much will depend on what supplies of soil are to hand (if any), whether it can be sterilized effectively, cost and quality of locally available materials.

Re-cycling Waste Compost
Re-cycling 'old' tomato and cucumber compost, after adjustment of pH and checking for soluble salts, is a procedure well worth consideration if a source exists. Such compost could have many uses including bedding plant production, although the 'risk' factor cannot be ignored.

Self-formulation or Purchase of Ready Mixed Composts?

It is up to every grower to decide whether it is economically sound to self-mix composts, providing all the equipment, raw materials and labour for doing so, or buy a 'tailored' compost. Obviously scale comes into things, as a small grower may find it uneconomic to buy in small quantities of formulated composts as he is unable to take in bulk supplies.

Self-formulation
Some of the considerations are as follows:
1 Clean sheds with cement floors.
2 Shredders for soil/peat.
3 Rotary mixers.
4 Accurate weighing, measuring facilities for bulk materials and additives (capital costs).
5 Sterilization facilities where soil is involved (capital costs).
6 Labour availability.
7 Storage under cover for raw materials and mixed compost.
8 Costing of whole exercise, in terms of capital, materials and labour, including management.
9 Quality and consistency of end product.
10 Scale of operation.

Bought in Composts
1 Unit price delivered.
2 Consistency of product.
3 Reliability of supplies (weather factors).
4 Alternative use of labour.
5 Avoidance of capital costs (not involved in compost mixing).
6 Scale of operation.

Chemicals Used in Composts

Chemical	Per bushel	Per cu yd	Per m^3
Ammonium Nitrate (35% N)	¼ oz – ¾ oz	5 oz–1 lb	200 g–600 g
Ammonium Nitrate Lime Nitro-chalk (25% N) Nitra-shell (34% N)	¼ oz– 2 oz	5 oz– 2½ lb	200 g–1600 g
Urea Formaldehyde (46% N)	¼ oz– 1½ oz	5 oz–2 lb	200 g–1200 g (1.2 kg)
Superphosphates (18–21% P_2O_5) Triple Superphosphates (47% P_2O_5)	½ oz– 2 oz	10 oz– 2 lb 8 oz	400g–1600 g (1.6 kg)
Potassium Nitrate (14%N – 46% K_2O)	½ oz– 2 oz	10 oz– 2 lb 8 oz	400g–1600 g (1.6 kg)
Potassium Sulphate (48% K_2O)	¼ oz– 2 oz	5 oz– 2 lb 8 oz	200g–1600g (1.6 kg)
Keizerite (17% magnesium) (Dolomitic Lime)	½ oz– 3 oz	10 oz– 4 lb	400g–2400g (2.4 kg)
Ground Limestone	¾ oz– 6 oz	1 lb–8 lbs	600g–4800 g (4.8 kg)
Frit WN255 or 253A	½ oz	10 oz	400 g

These are 'normal' rates for compost additions and their rate varies from seed sowing up to final potting – they are selected to give correct balance of nutrients.

Compost Formulae

John Innes Composts

John Innes Seed Compost
2 parts (by bulk) of Loam (sterilized by heat preferably)
1 part by bulk of Peat

178 **Composts**

1 part by bulk of Coarse Sand
to each bushel (22 × 10 × 10 in) add ¾ oz ground limestone (1 lb/cu yd/600 g/m^3) and 1½ oz superphosphates (30 oz/cu yd/1200 g/m^3).

John Innes Potting Compost
7 parts by bulk of Loam
3 parts by bulk of Peat
2 parts by bulk of Coarse Sand
For No. 1 compost, to each bushel add ¾ oz of ground limestone (1 lb/cu yd/500 g/m^3) and ¼ lb of John Innes Base Fertilizer (5¼ lb/cu yd/3.2 kg/m^3) (2 parts by weight Hoof and Horn Meal, 2 parts Superphosphates of Lime and 1 part Sulphate of Potash).
For No. 2 compost add 1½ oz of ground limestone (2 lb/cu yd/1200 g/m^3) and ½ lb base fertilizer (10.5 lb/cu yd/6.4 kg/m^3).
For No. 3 compost, add 2¼ oz of ground limestone (3 lbs/cu yd/1800 g/m^3) and ¾ lb base fertilizer (16 lbs/cu yd/9.6 kg/m^3).

Mixtures for Rooting Cuttings
There are no 'standard' mixes for rooting cuttings. It is normal to use 50/50 peat/sand plus lime with small fertilizer additions. The mix listed (see below) is ideal. Various mixtures of peat/perlite – peat/vermiculite etc., are also used.

Soilless Composts

Typical Formulae (See also Peat Blocking Composts)

Seed Sowing (and Rooting Cuttings), 50% Peat, 50% Sand, by Volume

	Per bushel	Per cu yd	Per m^3
Superphosphates (18%)	1–2 oz	1¼–2½ lb	800g–1.6 kg
Potassium Nitrate	½ oz	10 oz	400 g
Ground Limestone	4–6 oz	5–7½ lb	3.2 kg
*Sulphate of Potash	¼ oz	5 oz	200 g

*Optional – include for tomatoes

Pricking Out and Potting, 75% Peat, 25% Sand, by Volume

	Per bushel	Per cu yd	Per m³
Urea			
**Formaldehyde – Winter	¾ oz	1 lb	500 g
(Nitroform) – Spring	1 oz	1¼ lb	800 g
– Summer	1½ oz	2 lb	1000 g
Superphosphates (18%)	2 oz	2½ lb	1600 g
Potassium Nitrate	1 oz	1¼ lb	800 g
Sulphate of Potash (for tomatoes)	½ oz	¾ lb	400 g
Dolomitic Lime } Ground Limestone }	3 oz of each	4 lb of each	2.4 kg of each
Frit WM255 or 253A	¼ oz	10 oz	400 g
**Avoid if storage involved (more than 7 days). Include instead:			
Ammonium Nitrate	½ oz	10 oz	400 g

Base Fertilizers

Many growers now prefer to use 'prepared' base fertilizers, preferably slow-release. A slow release nutrient meters out the plant foods by depending on the breakdown of slow-release 'mechanism', size of particles, etc. – a procedure theoretically prone to upset by abrasion of the coated nutrient particle. To offset this danger recent developments are to hold the nutrient on a zeolitic clay/resin matrix – VITAX QS – which is likened to a currant bun with its intermix of clay/resin particles, with the simple coated particle as a toffee apple. *The release of nutrients by all types is very temperature dependent.*

A selection of the main types is as follows:

Ficote (Fisons Ltd.) (Formerly Nutricote)

Ficote is made from 3/4 mm granules of fertilizer. The basic principle involved in coating them is to blow or drop them so that they are free and moving in a current of air as in a prill tower. As all objects fall at the same rate the granules pass at a given speed through a spray web of polyolefin resin (PVC base). Since the granules are not in contact with one another they are coated as near to perfection as is possible. The release rate of nutrient from the granule is governed by the inclusion into the polyolefin resin of a water-soluble powder of a 1 micron grade. This is incorporated into the resin while it is in the molten state prior to spraying. *All coated fertilizers have their release governed by temperature.* In the case of Ficote the timed release is calculated at 25°C. That is to say that 80% of the nitrogen content will be released over the specified time period at a constant controlling temperature. Temperatures above or below this temperature either lengthen or shorten that term. Fisons claim greater safety to plants with the use of their product. It is available in various grades, used at rates from 1 lb to 4 lb according to suppliers' instructions. One month is the suggested storage period for formulated composts.

Osmocote
(Sierra U.K. Ltd., 5 Eldon Chambers, Wheelers Gate, Nottingham, NG1 2NS.)

Soluble fertilizers coated with resin – highly temperature dependent. There are six formulations with nutrient-release characteristics observed at a soil substrate temperature of 70°F (21°C). 8–9 month formulations (three weeks minimal release, then 0.4% per day for remainder of stated period).

1 8–9 month Regular (18–11–10)
2 8–9 month Fast Start (17–11–11) for summer potting
3 8–9 month Nitrogen (38–0–0) for specialized purposes
4 3–4 month Regular (15–12–15)
5 3–4 month High Nitrogen (18–11–11)
6 3–4 month Nitrogen (40–0–0)

Rate
Suppliers give full directions for use – (25% *less* being general for soil based composts).

Lime
With these products pH adjustment of compost is required, by adding ground limestone and dolomitic limestone at the *appropriate rate*, generally 4 lb per cubic yard (2.370 kg/m^3) *of each*, a total of 8 lb per cubic yard (4.8 kg/m^3) (approx. 3–6 oz per bushel). *Much less may be required for soil-based composts, depending on analysis. Peat-based composts are usually used at one pH below soil-based*, e.g. Soil 6–6.5, Peat 5–5.5.

Superphosphates
To provide early supplies of phosphates (on soilless composts especially), apply single superphosphates (18%) at 4 lb per cubic yard (2.4 kg/m^3) (approx. 3 oz per bushel).

Trace Elements
For soilless composts apply fritted trace elements at 10 oz per cubic yard (370 g per m^3) (½ oz per bushel approx.). (Not Vitax Products.) This may not be necessary with a good soil-based compost. For intensive culture it may be advisable, although experience will soon determine this.

Vitax QS Base – Vitax Q4
(Steetly Chemicals Ltd., incorporating Vitax Ltd., Liverpool Road, North Burscough, Ormskirk, Lancs L40 0SB)

As stated earlier, Vitax QS range of slow-release nutrients operate on a different basis to Ficote and Osmocote. They also contain a full range of trace elements, making the addition of fritted trace elements unnecessary. But pH adjustment with lime is required (but *not* applying dolomitic limestone as magnesium is contained in the QS range). The range is:

> QS1 12 month formulation for long-growth period subjects, e.g. shrubs, conifers, etc.
> QS2 9 month fertilizer. Pot plants of longer growing times.
> QS3 6 month fertilizer. For bedding plants, and shorter term items. Full instructions are available from the company.

Slow- Release Fertilizers (Not Coated)
A range of these is available, notably Vitax Q4 (Steetly Chemicals – see above) containing trace elements. The analysis is:

Nitrogen	5.30%
Phosphoric Acid (soluble)	6.80%
Phosphoric Acid (insoluble)	.70%
Potash	10.0%
Trace Elements:	
Magnesium	1.75%
Iron (chelate)	.25%
Manganese (chelate)	115ppm
Copper (chelate)	40ppm
Boron	20ppm
Molybdenum	1ppm

A higher nitrogen form is Q4 HN which has:

Nitrogen	10%
Phosphoric Acid (soluble)	6.80%
Phosphoric Acid (insoluble)	0.30%
Potash	10.20%

Trace element content as for Vitax Q4

Vitax Q4 and Q4 HN are both stable, which means that composts containing these can be stored for long periods.

pH Adjustment
This must take place before adding Q4 or Q4 HN, normal rates being 4–8 lb per cu yd (2.370 kg–4.713 kg/m^3) (3–6 oz per bushel) but lime requirement should always be checked by analysis.

182 Composts

Rates of Use/Seed Sowing and Cuttings
Both are used at rate of from 5–10 oz per cu yd (400–800 g per m^3) (½–1 oz per bushel) for small seed and cuttings; 10–20 oz per cu yd (800–1600 g per m^3) (1–2 oz per bushel) for larger seeds or cuttings.

Rates for Potting Composts
For pricking off and first potting, use at 3 kg per m^3 (4 oz per bushel) up to 6 kg per m^3 (8 oz per bushel). 'Soft' plants at final potting (tomatoes and chrysanthemums) can be given 7.5 kg per m^3 (10 oz per bushel).

In all cases quantities can be reduced where good loam and soils are used. (Analysis useful. Additions to proprietary composts must be done on a pro-rata basis according to compost type.)

Enmag
(S.A.I. Horticulture Ltd., Livingstone, West Lothian, Scotland)
Analysis:

Nitrogen	5.5%
Phosphate (soluble)	3.5%
Phosphate (insoluble)	17.0%
Potash	9.0%
Magnesium	8.0%

This is a 'slow release' fertilizer in a form not prone to leaching. It is added at rates as follows:
Subsequent to addition of lime for pH adjustment and fritted trace elements (253A) at 10 oz per cu yd (½ oz per bushel, 400 g per m^3).

Plantasan 4D
(Duphor–Midox Ltd., Smarden, Kent)
This is a complete slow-release fertilizer, of the following analysis:

> Nitrogen 20% – in slow, medium and fast-release form.
> Phosphate 10% – in slow-release form (P_2O_5).
> Potash 15% in slow *and* fast release form (K_2O).
> Magnesium – in slow release form (chloride free).
> Micro nutrients iron, manganese, boron, copper, zinc, cobalt, and molybdenum in chelated or non-chelated forms.

It is in two forms, coarse and fine, the latter (Fine 0.3 – 215 mn) being recommended mainly for glasshouse use. *Lime must be added to adjust pH.* Rates vary from ¾ lb/cu yd (½ kg/m^3) for seedlings up to 5 lb/cu yd (3 kg/m^3) for 'greedy crops'. Tomatoes and bedding plants are 3½ lb/cu yd/2 kg/m^3).

Composts

Note: These are examples of slow-release fertilizers to illustrate basic principles involved in their use as developed by manufacturers. Additional feeding will be required according to growth rate, and modern views are to use liquid feeds before there is any sign or hint of food exhaustion. **Always follow makers' instructions as the situation is a changing one.**

Costings

Only detailed consideration of existing circumstances, enquiry to compost and equipment suppliers for costs, etc., can give all the answers. Many larger organizations are able to come up with unit cost per pot or per box. When making these calculations, the following notes are useful.

Average Number of Pots Per Bushel, Cu Yd, M³ of Compost

Size of Pot		Pots Filled Per Bushel	Pots Filled per cu yd	Per m³
in	mm (approx.)			
2¼	58	370	7770	9990
2½	65	220	4620	5940
3	75	150	3150	4050
4	100	55	1155	1485
5	125	30	630	810
6	150	18	378	486

Note: These figures will vary according to compost type and firmness of potting so they can only be taken as a guide.

Number of Seed Trays Per Bushel, Cu Yd, M³ of Compost

Standard seed tray size – 2 × 9 × 15 in (5 × 23 × 38 cm) (external measurements). They may vary in size and depth. Each tray takes approx. 1/10th of a bushel, so:

    1 bushel = fills 8–10 trays
    1 cu yd = fills 180–210 trays
    1 m³ = fills 220–270 trays

Note: These are approximations.
For plant packs FYBA packs or pots or containers of various sizes, a trial run on a bushel basis will very quickly give quantities filled. Multiply by 21 for cu yd and 27 for cu m. Manufacturers can supply compost volume information. 'Jiffys' (7's and 9's) are bought by quantity not size.

Conversion Table

(rounded off figures in brackets)

Quantities of Chemical

Per bushel	Per cu yd	Per metre^3
¼ oz	5.2½ oz (5)	200 g
½ oz	10.5 oz (10)	400 g
¾ oz	15.7½ oz (1 lb)	600 g
1 oz	1¼ lb (20)	(800 g)
2 oz	42 oz (2½ lb)	1600 g (1.6 kg)
3 oz	(4 lb)	2400 g (2.4 kg)
4 oz	5¼ lb	3200 g (3.2 kg)
5 oz	(6½ lb)	4 kg
6 oz	(8 lb)	4.8 kg
7 oz	(9 lb)	5.6 kg
8 oz	(10.5 lb)	6.4 kg
9 oz	(12 lb)	7.2 kg
10 oz	(13 lb)	8 kg

bushel = 8 gallons = 36 litres
21 bushels per cu yd = 762 litres
27 bushels per cu m = 980 litres

Blocking Composts

There are many approaches to blocking composts. Early use of blocks centred round John Innes-type composts with extra loam for 'binding' the block. Now blocking composts are invariably 'blacker' types of sedge peat adjusted for pH if necessary and with 'slow-release' fertilizer incorporated. Dutch Poldersoil is also widely used in the Humberside area (U.K.). Most major peat firms provide either the peat for blocking or pre-formulated compost. Some of the larger central propagating firms such as Crystal Heart have their own supplies of peat specifically for blocking, having found that 'commercial' supplies of blocking composts do not meet their requirements.

Fertilizer Requirements of Peat Blocking Composts

	Low N Blocks		Winter Blocks (Approximately) (4.3 cm blocks)		Summer Blocks (7.5 cm blocks)			
	cu yd	kg/m^3	cu yd	kg/m^3	cu yd	kg/m^3	cu yd	kg/m^3
Constituents								
Ammonium nitrate	2½ oz	0.1	–	–	–	–	–	–
*Urea formaldehyde	5 oz	0.2	10 oz	0.4	10 oz	0.4	15 oz	0.6
**Potassium nitrate	–	–	1¼ lb	0.75	1½ lb	1.0	1½ lb	1.0
Normal superphosphate (18% P_2O_5)	2 lb	1.5	2 lb	1.5	2 lb	1.5	2 lb	1.5
Sulphate of potash	1¼ lb	0.75	–	–	–	–	–	–
Ground chalk	2¾ lb	2.25	2¾ lb	2.25	2¾ lb	2.25	2¾ lb	2.25
Magnesian limestone	2¾ lb	2.25	2¾ lb	2.25	2¾ lb	2.25	2¾ lb	2.25
Fritted trace elements (WM255A or 253A)	10 oz	0.4	10 oz	0.4	10 oz	0.4	10 oz	0.4

* Do not store compost for longer than 7 days
** Potassium nitrate can be replaced by an equal weight of potassium sulphate, plus one-third the amount of ammonium nitrate.

Practical Aspects of Mixing Composts

Material Handling

Measuring bulk or *mixed* composts, measuring lime and fertilizer additives and mixing this *uniformly* through the mix are essential points to note. Note that there is bulk loss on mixing peat due to pore space of peat or loam being filled with sand. This bulk loss is in the order of 15–20%, e.g. 3m^3 peat plus 3m^3 sand will *not* result in 6 m^3 of compost, but around 5 m^3. There can be many ways of organizing mixing from shovelling to mechanical handling, with tractor and bucket, to cement-type rotary mixers. Individual planning of the operation is essential but the volume of mix *must be known accurately before adding lime and fertilizers*. pH adjustment is generally on the basis of 1 lb of ground limestone per cu yd (300 g per m^3) of peat contained in the mix to give a difference of 0.3 of a pH unit, e.g. from pH 3.6 to pH 3.9 by 1 lb per cu yd (300 g per m^3). So to bring the pH up to 5.5 would require 5.5 – 3.6 = 1.9 difference $\frac{1.9}{3} = 6 \times 1$ lb = 6lb per cu yd or $\frac{1.9}{3} = 6 \times 300$ g = 1.8 kg per m^3.

Composts

Plant Per Acre/Ha
Note that this does not allow for areas lost by paths etc.

Spacing Imperial in	Spacing Metric cm	Plants/acre	Plants/hectare
6 × 6	15 × 15	174,000	429,954
6 × 10	15 × 25	105,000	259,455
8 × 8	20 × 20	98,000	242,158
8 × 10	20 × 25	78,000	192,738
10 × 10	25 × 25	63,000	155,673
11 × 6	27.5 × 15	95,000	234,745
11 × 8	27.5 × 20	91,000	224,867
11 × 10	27.5 × 25	57,000	140,847
12 × 6	30 × 15	87,000	214,977
12 × 8	30 × 20	65,000	160,675
12 × 10	30 × 25	52,000	128,492
12 × 12	30 × 30	44,000	108,724
18 × 6	45 × 15	58,000	143,318
18 × 9	45 × 22.5	39,000	96,369
18 × 12	45 × 30	29,000	71,659
18 × 18	45 × 45	19,000	46,949
24 × 12	60 × 30	22,000	54,362
24 × 18	60 × 45	14,500	35,829
24 × 24	60 × 60	10,900	26,933
30 × 12	75 × 30	17,400	42,995
30 × 18	75 × 45	11,600	28,663
30 × 24	75 × 60	8,700	21,497
30 × 30	75 × 75	7,000	17,297
36 × 18	90 × 45	9,700	23,968
36 × 24	90 × 60	7,300	18,038
36 × 30	90 × 75	5,800	14,331
36 × 36	90 × 90	4,800	11,860

Appendix

List of Firms Supplying Seeds

(V = Vegetables, F = Flowers)

Asmer Seeds Ltd.	VF	Asmer House, Ash Street, Leicester LE5 0DD.
Bejo Seeds Ltd.	V	PO Box 9, Noord-Scharwoude, Holland.
Breeders' Seeds Ltd.	VF	Summerwood Lane, Halsall, Nr. Ormskirk, Lancs L39 8RQ.
D. T. Brown & Co. Ltd.	VF	Station Road, Poulton-le-fylde, Blackpool FY6 7HX.
Bruinsma (Guernsey) Ltd.	V	Ennerdale, Les Pres Road, St. Peters, Guernsey.
Clause (UK) Ltd.	VF	Charvil Farm, New Bath Road, Charvil, Reading RG10 9RU.
Elsoms Seeds Ltd.	V	Spalding, Lincs PE11 1QG.
Enza Zaden de Enkuizer Zaadhamdel BV	V	PO Box 7, Paktuinen 21–23, 1600 AA Enkhuizen, Holland. UK address: D. Taylor, 31 Raleigh Road, Teignmouth, Devon.
Finney Lock Seeds Ltd.	VF	94–104 Grainger Street, Newcastle-upon-Tyne NE99 1PB.
Eddie Horrigan	VF	Culshaw Farm, Bescar Lane, Scarisbrick Ormskirk, Lancs.
Hurst Gunson Cooper Taber Ltd.	VF	Witham, Essex CM8 2DX.
E. W. King & Co. Ltd.	VF	Coggeshall, Colchester, Essex.
J. W. Moles & Son Ltd.	VF	Stanway, Colchester, Essex.

List of Firms Supplying Seeds

Nickerson Zwaan & Co. Ltd.	VF	Pelham Road, Grimsby, South Humberside DN 34 4SU.
Nunhems Zaden BV	VF	PO Box 4005, 6080 AA Haelen, Holland.
Pinetree Vandemburg	V	Lower Road, Effingham, Leatherhead, Surrey KT24 5JP.
Rijk Zwaan BV	V	De Lier (Holland) Burgem, Crezeelaan 40, PO Box 40, Holland UK address: G. Street, 42 Linden Way, Boston, Lincs.
Hans Rood	V	2280 CG Rijswijk, PO Box 1163, Holland..
Royal Sluis BV	VF	PO Box 22, 1600 AA Enkhuizen, Holland.
Charles Sharpe & Co. Ltd.	VF	Sleaford, Lincs NG34 7HA.
Sinclair McGill Ltd.	VF	Marsh Lane, Boston, Lincs.
Sluis en Gro BV	VF	Westeinde 62, PO Box 13, 1600 AA Enkhuizen, Holland.
A. R. Swaan & Co. Ltd.	VF	Yorkshire Bank Chambers, Bethleham St, Grimsby, Humberside ON31 1LA.
A. L. Tozer Ltd.	VF	Cobham, Surrey KT11 3EH.
Samuel Yates Ltd.	VF	The Seed Centre, Withyfold Drive, Macclesfield, Cheshire SK10 2BE.
Van der Ploeg's Elite Zaden BV	VF	2990 AA Barendrecht, Holland.
Van Staaveren	F	P. Smith, Rectory Lane, Ashington, West Sussex, RH20 3AS.

Acknowledgements

Individuals
W. Godley, South of Scotland Electricity Board, Hamilton, Scotland.
F. Hardy, West of Scotland Agricultural College, Auchincruive, Ayr.
J. Rendell, Agricultural Economics Department, University of Reading, Reading.

Papers and Articles

Fuels for Glasshouse Heating	Ministry of Agriculture, Fisheries and Food, May, 1979
The Grower, 50 Doughty Street, London WC1	Numerous references.
Nurseryman and Garden Centre, Horticulture Industry, Benn Bros. Ltd., Sovereign Way, Tonbridge, Kent	Numerous references.
G. C. & H. T. J., Haymarket Publishing Ltd., 38–42 Hampton Road, Teddington, Middlesex	Numerous references
R. H. S. Paxton Bursary I. G. Walls, 1960	Design cropping and economics of mobile greenhouses in Britain and the Netherlands

Books

Hydroponics	Dudley Harris	U.K. edition revised by A. M. Berrie and I. G. Walls, David and Charles, 1974

Acknowledgements

Making your Garden Pay	I. G. Walls and A. S. Horsburgh	David and Charles, 1974
The Complete Book of the Greenhouse	I. G. Walls	Ward Lock 1976 new edition, 1979
Tomato Growing Today	I. G. Walls	David and Charles, 1972 and 1977

Annual Reports, etc.

Agricultural Institute (Kinsealy), Malahide Road, Dublin	General data
Efford E. H. S., Lymington, Hampshire	Miscellaneous data
Fairfield E. H. S., Kirkham, Lancs. (now closed)	Miscellaneous data
Glasshouse Research Unit, West of Scotland Agricultural College, Auchincruive, Ayr.	Miscellaneous data
Glasshouse Crops Research Institute, Littlehampton, Sussex.	Miscellaneous data
Lee Valley E. H. S., Hoddesdon, Herts	Miscellaneous Data
Stockbridge House, E. H. S., Selby, Yorkshire	Data on rock wool culture, rhubarb etc.

Official Bodies

Agricultural Development Advisory Service (A.D.A.S.), Great Westminster House, Horseferry Road, London, SW1	Statistics, economic data, etc.
Electricity Council, Farm Electric Centre, National Agricultural Centre, Kenilworth, Warwickshire	General technical information

Acknowledgements

Institute of Agricultural Engineering (IMAG), Wageningen, Holland	Technical information
National Farmers Union of England, Agricultural House, Knightsbridge, London SW1	Statistics and official papers
National Farmers Union of Scotland, 17 Grosvenor Crescent, Edinburgh	Statistics and official papers
West of Scotland Agricultural College, Auchincruive, Ayr.	Various reports, technical leaflets, etc.

Firms

D. T. Brown & Co. Ltd., Station Road, Poulton-le-Fylde, Blackpool.	Technical data and use of material prepared for them by the author
Crystal Heart Salad Co. Ltd., Eastrington Road, Sandholme, Gilberdyke, Brough, North Humberside	General data
I.C.I. Plant Protection, Fernhurst, Haslemere, Surrey.	Data on N.F.T. systems
Jiffy Pot (U.K.) Ltd., Croft Chambers, Croft Road, Crowborough, E. Sussex	Technical information
Nutriculture Limited, Sandy Lane, Ormskirk, Lancashire	Data on N.F.T. systems

I am deeply grateful to D. T. Brown & Co., Seed Merchants, Station Road, Poulton-le-Fylde, Blackpool, for all the help and encouragement

192 Acknowledgements

they have afforded me in the writing of this book. In particular, I am grateful for their permission to use technical data which, as their consultant, I had compiled earlier for technical notes.

My thanks also to the seed trade in Britain and Holland for their help in various ways, also the horticultural industry in general.

I am exceptionally grateful to the Ministry of Agriculture & Fisheries for statistical data and the Agricultural Development Advisory Service (ADAS) which includes their research stations for much help and encouragement.

My thanks are also due to Guernsey State Research Station (R. Pollock) for considerable assistance and research data on roses and carnations in particular.

Finally I wish to thank Mr. Frank Hardy and his colleagues of the Horticultural Department, West of Scotland Agricultural College, Auchincruive, Scotland, for their helpful suggestions on the text.